Tennessee Williams

BABY DOLL
THE SCRIPT FOR THE FILM

SOMETHING UNSPOKEN
SUDDENLY LAST
SUMMER

PENGUIN BOOKS
IN ASSOCIATION WITH
MARTIN SECKER & WARBURG

Penguin Books Ltd, Harmondsworth, Middlesex, England
Penguin Books, 40 West 23rd Street, New York, New York 10010, U.S.A.
Penguin Books Australia Ltd, Ringwood, Victoria, Australia
Penguin Books Canada Ltd, 2801 John Street, Markham, Ontario, Canada L3R 1B4
Penguin Books (N.Z.) Ltd, 182–190 Wairau Road, Auckland 10, New Zealand

Baby Doll first published in Great Britain by Martin Secker & Warburg 1957
Published in Penguin Books 1957
Reprinted 1957, 1958
Copyright © the Estate of Tennessee Williams, 1956
Something Unspoken and *Suddenly Last Summer* first published as *The Garden District*
1958
First published in Great Britain by Martin Secker & Warburg 1959
Published in Penguin Books 1961
Copyright © the Estate of Tennessee Williams 1958
This collection first published in
Penguin Books 1968
Reprinted 1976, 1977, 1984

—

—

Printed in Great Britain by
Richard Clay (The Chaucer Press) Ltd,
Bungay, Suffolk
Set in Monotype Garamond

CONTENTS

BABY DOLL

For a number of years Elia Kazan, the director of several of Tennessee Williams' plays on Broadway as well as films, had been urging Mr Williams to weld into an original film story two of his early one-act plays which were, roughly, concerned with the same characters and situation. And in the summer of 1955, while he was travelling in Europe, Mr Williams wrote and dispatched to Mr Kazan a proposed script, quite different from the two short plays. With some changes this was filmed the following winter mainly in the Mississippi rural area which had been the original setting of the two short plays.

Although he had himself adapted several of his Broadway successes for films, this was Mr Williams' first original screen play. Many who came to read it, including his publishers, felt that although few 'shooting' scripts have ever been published, this one was publishable as it stood.

The film, *Baby Doll*, which was previously announced as *The Whip Hand* and *Mississippi Woman*, was produced and directed in the winter of 1955–1956 by Elia Kazan for Newtown Productions, Inc., and is presented by Warner Brothers. The principal roles are filled by Carroll Baker, Eli Wallach, Karl Malden, and Mildred Dunnock. The illustrations are from the film production and are reproduced by the kind permission of Warner Brothers.

1]

INTERIOR. DAY.
[*A voluptuous girl, under twenty, is asleep on a bed, with the covers thrown off. This is* BABY DOLL MEIGHAN, ARCHIE LEE'*s virgin wife. A sound is disturbing her sleep, a steady sound, furtive as a mouse scratching, she stirs, it stops, she settles again, it starts again. Then she wakes, without moving, her back to that part of the wall from which the sound comes.*]

2]

INTERIOR. DAY. CLOSE SHOT. BABY DOLL.
[*She is a little frightened of what sounds like a mouse in the woodwork and still doesn't sound like a mouse in the woodwork. Then a crafty look.*]

3]

INTERIOR. DAY. FULL SHOT.
[*She gets up, as the sound is continuing, and moves stealthily out of her room.*]

4]

HALL. DAY. FULL SHOT.
[*She comes out of her room and just as stealthily opens the door to an adjoining room and peeks in.*]

5]

CLOSE SHOT. BABY DOLL.
[*Astonished and angry at what she sees.*]

6]

WHAT SHE SEES. ARCHIE LEE MEIGHAN.
[*He is crouched over a section of broken plaster in the wall, enlarging a space between exposed boards with a penknife. Unshaven, black jowled, in sweaty pyjamas. On the bed table*

behind him is a half-empty bottle of liquor, an old alarm clock, ticking away, a magazine called Spicy Fiction, *and a tube of ointment. After a moment he removes the knife and bends to peer through the enlarged crack.*]

7]

CLOSE SHOT. BABY DOLL.
BABY DOLL: Archie Lee. You're a mess.

8]

ARCHIE LEE.
[*He recovers.*]

9]

BABY DOLL.
BABY DOLL: Y'know what they call such people? Peepin' Toms!

10]

FULL SHOT. ARCHIE LEE'S BEDROOM.
ARCHIE LEE: Come in here, I want to talk to you.
BABY DOLL: I know what you're going to say, but you can save your breath.
ARCHIE LEE: [*Interrupting*] We made an agreement....
BABY DOLL: You promised my daddy that you would leave me alone till I was ready for marriage....
ARCHIE: Well?
BABY DOLL: Well, I'm not ready for it yet....
ARCHIE: And I'm going crazy....
BABY DOLL: Well, you can just wait....
ARCHIE: We made an agreement that when you was twenty years old we could be man and wife in more than just in name only.
BABY DOLL: Well, I won't be twenty till November the seventh....
ARCHIE: Which is the day after tomorrow!

BABY DOLL: How about your side of that agreement – that you'd take good care of me? GOOD CARE OF ME! Do you remember that?! Now the Ideal Pay As You Go Plan Furniture Company is threatening to remove the furniture from this house. And every time I bring that up you walk away. . . .

ARCHIE: Just going to the window to get a breath of air. . . .

BABY DOLL: Now I'm telling you that if the Ideal Pay As You Go Plan Furniture Company takes those five complete sets of furniture out of this house then the understanding between us will be cancelled. Completely!

11]

ARCHIE LEE. AT WINDOW.

[*He is listening. We hear the distant sound of the Syndicate Cotton Gin. Like a gigantic distant throbbing heart-beat.* ARCHIE LEE *puts the window down. He crosses to the mirror, dolefully considers his appearance.*]

BABY DOLL: Yeah, just look at yourself! You're not exactly a young girl's dream come true, Archie Lee Meighan.

[*The phone rings downstairs. This sound is instantly followed by an outcry even higher and shriller.*]

BABY DOLL: Aunt Rose Comfort screams ev'ry time the phone rings.

ARCHIE: What does she do a damn fool thing like that for?

[*The phone rings again.* AUNT ROSE COMFORT *screams downstairs. The scream is followed by high breathless laughter. These sounds are downstairs. Archie Lee exits.*]

BABY DOLL: She says a phone ringing scares her.

12]

HALL.

[ARCHIE *lumbers over to a staircase, much too grand for the present style of the house, and shouts down to the old woman below.*]

ARCHIE: Aunt Rose Comfort, why don't you answer that phone?

13]

DOWNSTAIRS HALL.

[AUNT ROSE *comes out of the kitchen and walks towards the hall telephone, withered hand to her breast.*]

AUNT ROSE: I cain't catch m'breath, Archie Lee. Phone give me such a fright.

ARCHIE: [*From above*] Answer it.

[*She has recovered some now and gingerly lifts the receiver.*]

AUNT ROSE: Hello? This is Miss Rose Comfort McCorkle speaking. No, the lady of the house is Mrs Archie Lee Meighan, who is the daughter of my brother that passed away ...

[ARCHIE LEE *is hurrying down the stairs.*]

ARCHIE: They don't wanta know that! Who in hell is it talking and what do they want?

AUNT ROSE: I'm hard of hearing. Could you speak louder, please? The what? The Ideal Pay As –

[*With amazing, if elephantine, speed,* ARCHIE *snatches the phone from the old woman.*]

ARCHIE: Gi'me that damn phone. An' close the door.

[*The old woman utters her breathless cackle and backs against the door.* ARCHIE *speaks in a hoarse whisper.*]

ARCHIE: Now what is this? Aw. Uh-huh. Today!? Aw. You gotta g'me more time. Yeah, well you see I had a terrible setback in business lately. The Syndicate Plantation built their own cotton gin and're ginnin' out their own cotton, now, so I lost their trade and it's gonna take me a while to recover from that. . . .

[*Suddenly*]

Then TAKE IT OUT! TAKE IT OUT! Come and get th' damn stuff. And you'll never get my business again! Never!

[*They have hung up on him. He stands there – a man in tough trouble. Then abruptly starts massaging his exhausted head of hair.*]

AUNT ROSE: [*Timidly*] Archie Lee, honey, you all aren't going to lose your furniture, are you?

ARCHIE: [*Hoarse whisper*] Will you shut up and git on back in the kitchen and don't speak a word that you heard on the phone, if you heard a word, to my wife! And don't holler no more in this house, and don't cackle no more in it either, or by God I'll pack you up and haul you off to th' county home at Sunset.

AUNT ROSE: What did you say, Archie Lee, did you say something to me?

ARCHIE: Yeah. I said shoot. [*He starts upstairs.*]

[AUNT ROSE *cackles uneasily and enters the kitchen. Suddenly, we hear another scream from her. We pan with her, and reveal* OLD FUSSY, *the hen, on top of the kitchen table pecking the corn bread.*]

14]

UPSTAIRS HALL.

[ARCHIE *is heading back to his bedroom.* BABY DOLL *appears in a flimsy wrapper at the turn of the stairs crossing to the bathroom.*]

BABY DOLL: What made her holler this time?

ARCHIE: How in hell would I know what made that ole woman holler this time or last time or the next time she hollers?

BABY DOLL: Last time she hollered it was because you throwed something at her.

[*She enters bathroom.* ARCHIE LEE *stands in doorway.*]

ARCHIE: What did I ever throw at Aunt Rose Comfort?

BABY DOLL: [*From inside bathroom*] Glass a water. Fo' singin' church hymns in the kitchen. . . .

[*We hear the shower go on.*]

ARCHIE: This much water! Barely sprinkled her with it! To catch her attention. She don't hear nothing, you gotta do somethin' to git the ole woman's attention.

[*On an abrupt impulse he suddenly enters the bathroom. Sounds of a struggle. The shower.*]

BABY DOLL: Keep y'r hands off me! Will yuh? Keep your hands off . . . Off.

[ARCHIE LEE *comes out of the bathroom good and wet. The*

shower is turned off. BABY DOLL'S *head comes out past the door.*]

BABY DOLL: I'm going to move to the Kotton King Hotel, the very next time you try to break the agreement! The very next time!
[*She disappears....*]

15]

CLOSE SHOT. ARCHIE LEE WET.

DISSOLVE.

16]

ARCHIE LEE.
[*He is seated in his 1937* Chevy Sedan. *The car is caked with pale-brown mud and much dented. Pasted on the windshield is a photo of* BABY DOLL *smiling with bewilderment at the birdie-in-the-camera.*

ARCHIE LEE *is honking his horn with unconcealed and un-modified impatience.*]

ARCHIE: [*Shouting*] Baby Doll! Come on down here, if you're going into town with me. I got to be at the doctor's in ten minutes. [*No answer*] Baby Doll!!!
[*From inside the house.* BABY DOLL'S *voice.*]

BABY DOLL: If you are so impatient, just go ahead without me. Just go ahead. I know plenty of ways of getting downtown without you.

ARCHIE: You come on.
[*Silence. The sound of the Syndicate Gin.* ARCHIE *does a sort of imitation. His face is violent.*]

ARCHIE: Baby Doll!!!
[BABY DOLL *comes out on the sagging porch of the mansion. She walks across the loose boards of the porch through stripes of alternate light and shadow from the big porch pillars. She is humming a little cakewalk tune, and she moves in sympathy to it. She has on a skirt and blouse, white, and skintight, and pearl chokers the size of golf balls seen from a medium distance. She draws up beside the car and goes no farther.*]

ARCHIE: You going in town like that?

BABY DOLL: Like what?

ARCHIE: In that there outfit. For a woman of your modest nature that squawks like a hen if her *husband* dast to put his hand on her, you sure do seem to be advertising your –

BABY DOLL: [*Drowning him out*] My figure has filt out a little since I bought my trousseau AND paid for it with m'daddy's insurance money. I got two choices, wear clo'se skintight or go naked, now which do you want me t' –

ARCHIE:
    [*Aw, now, hell! Will you git into th' car?*
    Their loud angry voices are echoed by the wandering poultry.]

BABY DOLL: I will git into the rear seat of that skatterbolt when you git out of the front seat and walk around here to open the door for me like a gentleman.

ARCHIE: Well, you gonna wait a long time if that's what you're waiting for!

BABY DOLL: I vow my father would turn over in his grave. . . .

ARCHIE: I never once did see your father get out and open a car door for your mother or any other woman. . . . Now get on in. . . .
    [*She wheels about and her wedgies clack-clack down the drive. At foot of drive she assumes a hitch-hiker's stance. A hot-rod skids to a sudden and noisy stop. ARCHIE LEE bounds from his car like a jack rabbit, snatching a fistful of gravel as he plummets down drive. Hurls gravel at grinning teen-age kids in hot-rod, shouting incoherently as they shoot off, plunging BABY DOLL and her protector in a dust-cloud. Through the dust . . .*]

ARCHIE LEE: Got your licence number you pack a –

DISSOLVE.

16A]

THE CAR INTERIOR.
    [*They are jolting down the road.*]

ARCHIE: Baby Doll, y'know they's no torture on earth to equal the torture which a cold woman inflicts on a man that

17

she won't let touch her??!! No torture to compare with it! What I've done is!! Staked out a lot in hell, a lot with a rotten house on it and five complete sets of furniture not paid for....

BABY DOLL: What you done is bit off more'n you can chew.

ARCHIE: People know the situation between us. Yestiddy on Front Street a man yelled to me, 'Hey Archie Lee, has y'wife outgrowed the crib yet??' And three or four others haw-hawed! Public! Humiliation!

[BABY DOLL *in back seat, her beads and earrings ajingle like a circus pony's harness.*]

BABY DOLL: Private humiliation is just as painful.

ARCHIE: Well! – There's an agreement between us! You ain't gonna sleep in no crib tomorrow night, Baby, when we celebrate your birthday.

BABY DOLL: If they remove those five complete sets of furniture from the house, I sure will sleep in the crib because the crib's paid for – I'll sleep in the crib or on the top of Aunt Rose Comfort's pianner....

ARCHIE: And I want to talk to you about Aunt Rose Comfort.... I'm not in a position to feed and keep her any –

BABY DOLL: Look here, Big Shot, the day Aunt Rose Comfort is unwelcome under your roof ...

ARCHIE: Baby Doll, honey, we just got to unload ourselves of all unnecessary burdens.... Now she can't cook and she –

BABY DOLL: If you don't like Aunt Rose Comfort's cookin', then get me a regular servant. I'm certainly not going to cook for a fat ole thing like you, money wouldn't pay me – Owwwww!

[ARCHIE *has backhanded her. And prepares to do so again.*]

BABY DOLL: Cut that out....

ARCHIE: You better quit saying 'fat ole thing' about me!

BABY DOLL: Well, you get young and thin and I'll quit calling you a fat old thing. – What's the matter now?

[ARCHIE LEE *points to off right with a heavily tragic gesture.*]

TRAVELLING SHOT. SYNDICATE GIN.
THEIR VIEWPOINT.
> [*It is new, handsome, busy, clearly prospering. A sign (large)
> reads:* SYNDICATE COTTON GIN.]

18]

TWO SHOT. ARCHIE AND BABY DOLL.
ARCHIE: There it is! There it is!
BABY DOLL: Looks like they gonna have a celebration!
ARCHIE: Why shouldn't they!!?? They now got every last
bit of business in the county, including every last bit of
what I used to get.
BABY DOLL: Well, no wonder, they got an up-to-date plant –
not like that big pile of junk you got!!
> [ARCHIE *glares at her.*]

QUICK DISSOLVE.

19]

WAITING-ROOM. DOCTOR'S OFFICE.
> [ARCHIE *and* BABY DOLL *enter, and he is still hotly pursuing
> the same topic of discussion.*]
ARCHIE: Now I'm just as fond of Aunt Rose Comfort –
BABY DOLL: You ain't just as fond of Aunt –
ARCHIE: Suppose she breaks down on us?? Suppose she gets
a disease that lingers –
> [BABY DOLL *snorts.*]
ARCHIE: All right, but I'm serving you notice. If that ole
woman breaks down and dies on my place, I'm not going
to be stuck with her funeral expenses. I'll have her burned
up, yep, cremated, cremated, is what they call it. And pack
her ashes in an ole Coca-Cola bottle and pitch the bottle
into TIGER TAIL BAYOU!!!
BABY DOLL: [*Crossing to inner door*] Doctor John? Come out
here and take a look at my husband. I think a mad dawg's
bit him. He's gone ravin' crazy!!

RECEPTIONIST: [*Appearing*] Mr Meighan's a little bit late for his appointment, but the doctor will see him.

BABY DOLL: Good! I'm going down to the –

ARCHIE: Oh, no, you're gonna sit here and wait till I come out. . . .

BABY DOLL: Well, maybe . . .

[ARCHIE *observes that she is exchanging a long, hard stare with a young man slouched in a chair.*]

ARCHIE: And look at this! Or somethin'.

[*He thrusts a copy of* Screen Secrets *into her hands and shoves her into a chair. Then glares at the young man, who raises his copy of* Confidential.]

DISSOLVE.

20]

INNER OFFICE.

[ARCHIE LEE *has been stripped down to the waist. The doctor has just finished examining him. From the ante-room, laughter, low. Which seems to make* ARCHIE LEE *nervous.*]

DOCTOR: You're not an old man, Archie Lee, but you're not a young man, either.

ARCHIE: That's the truth.

DOCTOR: How long you been married?

ARCHIE: Just about a year now.

DOCTOR: Have you been under a strain? You seem terrible nervous?

ARCHIE: No strain at all! None at all. . . .

[*Sound of low laughter from the waiting-room. Suddenly,* ARCHIE LEE *rushes over and opens the door.* BABY DOLL *and the* YOUNG MAN *are talking. He quickly raises his magazine. . . . Archie closes . . . the door, finishes dressing. . . .*]

DOCTOR: What I think you need is a harmless sort of sedative. . . .

ARCHIE: Sedative! Sedative! What do I want with a sedative???

[*He bolts out of the office. . . .*]

DISSOLVE.

21]

MEDIUM LONG SHOT. ARCHIE LEE'S CAR GOING DOWN FRONT STREET.

[BABY DOLL *sits on her side aloof. Suddenly a moving van passes the other way. On its side is marked the legend,* IDEAL PAY AS YOU GO PLAN FURNITURE COMPANY. *Suddenly,* BABY DOLL *jumps up and starts waving her hand, flagging the van down, then when this fails, flagging* ARCHIE LEE *down.*]

22]

CLOSER SHOT. ARCHIE'S CAR.

BABY DOLL: That was all our stuff!

ARCHIE: No it wasn't. . . .

BABY DOLL: That was our stuff. Turn around, go after them.

ARCHIE: Baby Doll, I've got to wait down here for my per-scription. . . .

[*At this moment another* IDEAL PAY AS YOU GO PLAN FURNITURE COMPANY *goes by, in the* OTHER *direction.*]

BABY DOLL: There goes another one, towards our house.

ARCHIE: Baby, let's go catch the show at the Delta Brilliant.

BABY DOLL: [*Starts beating him.*]

ARCHIE: Or let's drive over to the Flaming Pig and have some barbecue ribs and a little cold beer.

BABY DOLL: That's our stuff . . . !

[ARCHIE LEE *looks the other way.*]

I said that's our stuff . . . !! I wanta go home. HOME. NOW. If you don't drive me home now, I'll I'll, I'll – Mr Hanna. Mr Gus Hanna. You live on Tiger Tail Road . . .

ARCHIE: I'll drive you home.

[*He spins the car around and they start home.*]

23]

EXTERIOR MEIGHAN HOUSE. DAY.

[MEIGHAN'S *car turns in the drive. The van we saw is backed up to the house, and furniture is being removed from the house.* BABY DOLL *runs among them and starts to beat the movers.*]

They go right on with their work, paying no attention. After a time AUNT ROSE *puts her arms around* BABY DOLL *and leads her into the house.*]

24]

CLOSE SHOT. ARCHIE LEE.
[*He really is on a spot. Again he hears the sound of the Syndicate Cotton Gin. He makes the same sound, imitating it, he made earlier. He looks in its direction and spits. Then he gets out of the car and walks towards his empty home.*]

25]

INTERIOR. ARCHIE LEE'S HOUSE.
THE PARLOUR.
[BABY DOLL *is sobbing by the window. The screen door creaks to admit the hulking figure of* ARCHIE LEE.]

ARCHIE: [*Approaching*] Baby Doll. . . .

BABY DOLL: Leave me alone in here. I don't want to sit in the same room with a man that would make me live in a house with no furniture.

ARCHIE: Honey, the old furniture we got left just needs to be spread out a little. . . .

BABY DOLL: My daddy would turn in his grave if he knew, he'd turn in his grave.

ARCHIE: Baby Doll, if your daddy turned in his grave as often as you say he'd turn in his grave, that old man would plough up the graveyard.

[*Somewhere outside* AUNT ROSE *is heard singing; 'Rock of Ages'.*]

ARCHIE: She's out there pickin' roses in the yard just as if nothing at all had happened here. . . .

BABY DOLL: I'm going to move to the Kotton King Hotel. I'm going to move to the Kotton King Hotel. . . .

ARCHIE: No, you ain't, Baby Doll.

BABY DOLL: And I'm going to get me a job. The manager of the Kotton King Hotel carried my daddy's coffin, he'll give me work.

ARCHIE: What sort of work do you think you could do, Baby Doll?

BABY DOLL: I could curl hair in a beauty parlour or polish nails in a barber-shop, I reckon, or I could be a hostess and smile at customers coming into a place.

ARCHIE: What place?

BABY DOLL: Any place! I could be a cashier.

ARCHIE: You can't count change.

BABY DOLL: I could pass out menus or programmes or something and say hello to people coming in! [*Rises*] I'll phone now. [*She exits.*]

26]

HALL.

    [BABY DOLL *crosses to the telephone. She is making herself attractive as if preparing for an interview.*]

BABY DOLL: Kotton King? This is Mrs Meighan. I want to reserve a room for tomorrow mornin' and I want to register under my maiden name, which is Baby Doll Carson. My daddy was T. C. Carson who died last summer when I got married and he is a very close personal friend of the manager of the Kotton King Hotel – you know – what's his name. . . .

27]

EXTERIOR OF HOUSE.

    [ARCHIE *comes out door and wanders into the yard, passing* AUNT ROSE, *who holds a bunch of roses.*]

AUNT ROSE: Archie Lee, look at these roses! Aren't they poems of nature?

ARCHIE: Uh-huh, poems of nature.

    [*He goes past her, through the front gate and over to his Chevy. The front seat on the driver's side has been removed and a broken-down commodious armchair put in its place.*

    Sound of the Syndicate Gin, throbbing. ARCHIE LEE *reaches under the chair and fishes out a pint bottle. He takes a slug,*

23

listens to the Syndicate, takes another. Then he throws the bottle out of the car, turns the ignition key of the car and . . .]

28]

THE CHEVY ROCKS OUT OF THE YARD.

DISSOLVE.

29]

THE INTERIOR. BRITE SPOT CAFE.

[*A habitually crowded place. Tonight it is empty. In the corner a customer or two. Behind the bar, the man in the white apron with nothing to do is sharpening a frog gig on a stone. Enter* ARCHIE, *goes over to the bar.*]

ARCHIE: Didn't get to the bank today, Billy, so I'm a little short of change. . . .

[*The* BARTENDER *has heard this before. He reaches to a low shelf and takes out an unlabelled bottle and pours* ARCHIE *a jolt.*]

ARCHIE: Thanks. Where's everybody?

BARTENDER: Over to the Syndicate Gin. Free liquor over there tonight. Why don't you go over? [*Then he laughs sardonically.*]

ARCHIE: What's the occasion?

BARTENDER: First anniversary. Why don't you go over and help them celebrate.

ARCHIE: I'm not going to my own funeral either.

BARTENDER: I might as well lock up and go home. All that's coming in here is such as you.

ARCHIE: What you got there?

[*The* BARTENDER *holds up a frog gig. The ends, where just sharpened, glisten.*]

ARCHIE: Been getting any frogs lately?

BARTENDER: Every time I go out. Going tomorrow night and get me a mess. You wanna come? There's a gang going. You look like you could use some fresh meat.

[*Another rather despondent-looking character comes in.*]

ARCHIE: Hey, Mac, how you doing?

24

MAC: Draggin', man.

BARTENDER: Why ain't you over to the Syndicate like everybody else?

MAC: What the hell would I do over that place... That place
ruined me ... ruined me. ...

BARTENDER: The liquor's running free over there tonight.
And they got fireworks and everything. ...

MAC: Fireworks! I'd like to see the whole place up in smoke.
[*Confidentially*] Say, I'm good for a couple, ain't I?

> *As the* BARTENDER *reaches for the same bottle-without-a-
> label, we*

DISSOLVE TO

30]

EXTERIOR. SYNDICATE GIN.

> [*A big platform has been built for the celebration and decked out
> with flags, including the Stars and Bars of Dixie and the
> Mississippi State Banner.*
>
> *A band is playing 'Mississippi Millions Love You', the state
> song, which is being sung by an emotional spinster. Several public
> officials are present, not all of them happy to be there as the
> county has a strongly divided attitude towards the Syndicate-
> owned plantation. Some old local ward heeler is reeling onto the
> speaker's platform and a signal is given to stop the band music.
> THE OLD BOY lifts a tin cup, takes a long swallow and
> remarks.*]

THE OLD BOY: Strongest branch water that ever wet my
whistle. Must of come out of Tiger Tail Bayou.

> [*There is a great haw-haw.*]

THE OLD BOY: [*Continues*] Young man? Mr Vacarro. This is
a mighty fine party you're throwing tonight to celebrate
your first anniversary as superintendent of the Syndicate
Plantation and Gin. And I want you to know that all of us
good neighbours are proud of your achievement, bringin'
in the biggest cotton crop ever picked off the blessed soil of
Two River County.

> [*The camera has picked up a handsome, cocky young Italian,*

SILVA VACARRO. *His affability is not put on, but he has a way of darting glances right and left as he chuckles and drinks beer which indicates a certain watchfulness, a certain reserve.*

The camera has also picked up, among the other listeners, some uninvited guests ... including ARCHIE LEE *and his friend from the Brite Spot.* ARCHIE LEE *is well on the way and, of course, his resentment and bitterness are much more obvious.*]

THE OLD BOY: Now when you first come here, well, we didn't know you yet and some of us old-timers were a little standoffish, at first.

[VACARRO's *face has suddenly gone dark and sober. In his watchfulness he has noticed the hostile guests. With a sharp gesture of his head, he summons a man who works for him –* ROCK *– who comes up and kneels alongside. The following colloquy takes place right through* THE OLD BOY's *lines.*]

SILVA: There's a handful of guys over there that don't look too happy to me. . . .

ROCK: They got no reason to be. You put 'em out of business when you built your own gin, and started to gin your own cotton.

SILVA: Watch 'em, keep an eye on 'em, specially if they start to wander around. . . .

THE OLD BOY: [*Who has continued*] Natchully, a thing that is profitable to some is unprofitable to others. We all know that some people in this county have suffered some financial losses due in some measure to the success of the Syndicate Plantation.

[VACARRO *is looking around again. Rather defiantly, but at no one in particular. Between the knees of his corduroy riding breeches is a whip that he carries habitually, a braided leather riding crop.*]

THE OLD BOY: But as a whole, the community has reaped a very rich profit.

[*He has said this rather defiantly as if he knew he was bucking a certain tide. . . . A voice from the crowd.*]

VOICE: Next time you run for office you better run on the Republican ticket. Git the nigger vote, Fatso!

THE OLD BOY: [*Answering*] Just look at the new construction been going on! Contractors, carpenters, lumbermen, not to mention the owner and proprietor of the Brite Spot down the road there! And not to mention –

[*Suddenly somebody throws something at the speaker, something liquid and sticky. Instantly,* ROCK *and* VACARRO *spring up....*]

ROCK: Who done that?!?!

SILVA: [*Crossing to front of platform*] If anybody's got anything to throw, well, here's your target, here's your standing target! The wop! The foreign wop!!

[*Big rhubarb.* THE OLD BOY *is wiping his face with a wad of paper napkins.*

Suddenly, we see that something in the middle distance is on fire. The wide dark fields begin to light up. Voices cry alarm. Shouts, cries. Everyone and everything is lit by the shaking radiance of the fire.

VACARRO *races towards the fire. It is in the gin building. The volatile dust explodes. Loaded wagons are being pushed away, by Negro field-hands driven by* VACARRO.

A fire engine arrives. But it seems lax in its efforts and inefficient. A hose is pulled out, but there is insufficient water to play water on the blaze, and the hose itself falls short. The firemen are not merely ineffectual. Some seem actually indifferent. In fact, some of their faces express an odd pleasure in the flames, which they seem more interested in watching than fighting.

VACARRO *rushes among them exhorting, commanding, constantly gesturing with his short riding crop. In his frenzy, he lashes the crop at the man holding the fire hose. The man, resentfully, throws the end of the hose at* VACARRO, *who seizes the nozzle and walks directly towards and into the flames. Now men try to stop him.* VACARRO *turns the hose on them, driving them back and then goes into the flames. He disappears from sight. All we hear is his shouts in a foreign tongue. A wall collapses.*

The hose suddenly leaps about as if it has been freed. The crowd. Horrified. Then they see something.... VACARRO *comes out. He holds aloft a small, gallon-size kerosene can. He strikes at his trouser bottoms, which are hot. He is on the point of collapse.*

Men rush to him and drag him to a safe distance. He clutches the can.
They lay him out, and crouch around him. He is smudged and singed. His eyes open, look around.
His viewpoint. From this distorted angle, lit by the victorious flames are a circle of faces which are either indifferent or downright unfriendly. Some cannot control a faint smile.
VACARRO *clutches the can, closes his eyes.*
Another wall collapses.]

DISSOLVE.

31]

EXTERIOR. ARCHIE LEE'S HOUSE. NIGHT.
[ARCHIE LEE'*s car turns into the drive. He descends noiselessly as a thief. Camera follows him, and it and he discover* BABY DOLL *on the porch swing. There are several suitcases, packed and ready to go. In a chair near the porch swing, sleeping as mildly as a baby, is* AUNT ROSE COMFORT]

ARCHIE: What are you doin' out here at one o'clock in the morning?

BABY DOLL: I'm not talking to you.

ARCHIE: What are you doing out here?

BABY DOLL: Because in the first place, I didn't have the money to pay for a hotel room, because you don't give me any money, because you don't have any money, and secondly, because if I had the money I couldn't have no way of getting there because you went off in the Chevy, and leave me no way of getting anywhere, including to the fire which I wanted to see just like everyone else.

ARCHIE: What fire you talking about?

BABY DOLL: What fire am I talking about?

ARCHIE: I don't know about no fire.

BABY DOLL: You must be crazy or think I'm crazy. You mean to tell me you don't know the cotton gin burned down at the Syndicate Plantation right after you left the house.

ARCHIE: [*Seizing her arm*] Hush up. I never left this house.

28

BABY DOLL: You certainly did leave this house. ow!!

ARCHIE: Look here! Listen to what I tell you. I never left this house. . . .

BABY DOLL: You certainly did and left me here without a coke in the place. oww!! Cut it out!!

ARCHIE: Listen to what I tell you. I went up to bed with my bottle after supper –

BABY DOLL: What bed! ow!

ARCHIE: And passed out dead to the world. You got that in your haid?? Will you remember that now?

BABY DOLL: Let go my arm!

ARCHIE: What did I do after supper?

BABY DOLL: You know what you did, you jumped in the Chevy an' disappeared after supper and didn't get back till just – owww!!! Will you quit twisting my arm?

ARCHIE: I'm trying to wake you up. You're asleep, you're dreaming! What did I do after supper?

BABY DOLL: Went to bed! Leggo! Went to bed. Leggo! Leggo!

ARCHIE: That's right. Make sure you remember. I went to bed after supper and didn't wake up until I heard the fire whistle blow and I was too drunk to git up and drive the car. Now come inside and go to bed.

BABY DOLL: Go to what bed? I got no bed to go to!

ARCHIE: You will tomorrow. The furniture is coming back tomorrow.

[BABY DOLL *whimpers*.]

ARCHIE: [*Continues*] Did I hurt my little baby's arm?

BABY DOLL: Yais.

ARCHIE: Where I hurt little baby's arm?

BABY DOLL: Here. . . .

ARCHIE: [*He puts a big wet kiss on her arm*] Feel better?

BABY DOLL: No. . . .

ARCHIE: [*Another kiss. This travels up her arm*] My sweet baby doll. My sweet little baby doll.

BABY DOLL: [*Sleepily*] Hurt. . . . MMMMmmmm! Hurt.

ARCHIE: Hurt?

BABY DOLL: Mmm!

ARCHIE: Kiss?

BABY DOLL: Mmmmmmmmm!

ARCHIE: Baby sleepy?

BABY DOLL: MMMMMMM!

ARCHIE: Kiss good. . . .?

BABY DOLL: Mmmmm. . . .

ARCHIE: Make little room. . . . good. . . .

BABY DOLL: Too hot.

ARCHIE: Make a little room, go on. . . .

BABY DOLL: Mmmm. . . .

ARCHIE: Whose baby? Big sweet. . . . whose baby?

BABY DOLL: You hurt me. . . . Mmmm. . . .

ARCHIE: Kiss. . . .

[*He lifts her wrist to his lips and makes gobbling sound. We get an idea of what their courtship – such as it was – was like. Also how passionately he craves her, willing to take her under any conditions, including fast asleep.*]

BABY DOLL: Stop it. . . . Silly. . . . Mmmmmm. . . .

ARCHIE: What would I do if you was a big piece of cake?

BABY DOLL: Silly.

ARCHIE: Gobble! Gobble!

BABY DOLL: Oh you. . . .

ARCHIE: What would I do if you was angel food cake? Big white piece with lots of nice thick icin'?

BABY DOLL: [*Giggling now, in spite of herself. She's also sleepy*] Quit.

ARCHIE: [*As close as he's ever been to having her*] Gobble! Gobble! Gobble!

BABY DOLL: Archie!

ARCHIE: Hmmmmm. . . . [*He's working on her arm*] Skrunch, gibble, ghrumpt . . . etc.

BABY DOLL: You tickle. . . .

ARCHIE: Answer little question. . . .

BABY DOLL: What?

ARCHIE: [*Into her arm*] Where I been since supper?

BABY DOLL: Off in the Chevy –

[*Instantly he seizes her wrist again. She shrieks. The romance is over.*]

ARCHIE: Where I been since supper?

BABY DOLL: Upstairs. . . .

ARCHIE: Doing what?

BABY DOLL: With your bottle. Archie, leggo. . . .

ARCHIE: And what else. . . .

BABY DOLL: Asleep. Leggo. . . .

ARCHIE: [*Letting go*] Now you know where I been and what I been doing since supper. In case anybody asks.

BABY DOLL: Yeah.

ARCHIE: Now go to sleep. . . .

[*He seizes her suitcases and goes off into the house.* BABY DOLL *follows, and* AUNT ROSE *follows her, asleep on her feet. As they go in,* ARCHIE LEE *comes out and looks around. Then he listens.*]

ARCHIE: Nice quiet night. Real nice and quiet.

[*The gin can no longer be heard.*]

CUT TO

32]

BRITE SPOT CAFE. EXTERIOR. NIGHT.

[*It's not quiet here at all. The area in front of the entrance is crowded with cars. A holiday mood prevails. It's as if the fire has satisfied some profound and basic hunger and left the people of that community exhilarated.*

The pick-up truck of SILVA VACARRO *drives up, shoots into a vacant spot. He leaps from the driver's cab. He has not yet washed, his shirt is torn and blackened and he has a crude bandage around the arm that holds the whip. He stands for a few moments beside his truck, looking around at the cars, trying to find the car of the* MARSHAL, *which would indicate that that county official is inside. Then he sees what he's looking for. He walks over to the car which has the official seal on its side, and not finding the* MARSHAL *there, turns and strides into the . . .*]

33]

INTERIOR. BRITE SPOT. (A JUKE JOINT)

[*Everybody is talking about the fire. The juke box is a loud one. There are some dancing couples.*

SILVA VACARRO *passes by a little knot of men. He is followed by* ROCK, *holding the kerosene can. The camera stays with them. They smile.*]

A MAN: That ole boy is really burning!

[*One of the men detaches himself and moves in the direction that* VACARRO *took. Then another follows.*]

34]

GROUP OF MEN AROUND THE MARSHAL.

MARSHAL: What makes you think your gin was set fire to?

SILVA: Look around you. Did you ever see such a crowd of happy faces, looks like a rich man's funeral with all his relations attending.

MARSHAL: I'd hate to have to prove it.

SILVA: I'd hate to have to depend on you to prove it.

[*The man from the other group walks up.*]

MAN: What are you going to do about ginning out your cotton?

SILVA: I'll truck it over to Sunset. Collins'll gin it out for me.

MAN: Collins got cotton of his own to gin.

SILVA: Then I'll truck it across the river. Ain't nobody around here's gonna gin it.

MAN: I'm all set up to do it for you.

SILVA: I wouldn't give you the satisfaction.

[*The men drift back a few steps.*]

MARSHAL: [*He speaks a little for the benefit of the men in the room*] I honestly can't imagine if it was a case of arson who could of done it since every man jack that you put out of business was standing right there next to the platform when the fire broke out.

ROCK: One wasn't. I know one that wasn't.

MARSHAL: [*Wheeling on bar-stool to face him. Sharply*] Looky here, boy! Naming names is risky, just on suspicion.

ROCK: I didn't name his name. I just said I know it. And the initials are stamped on this here can.

MARSHAL: [*Quickly*] Let's break it up, break it up, not the time or the place to make accusations, I'll take charge of this can. I'll examine it carefully to see if there's any basis for thinking it was used to start a fire with.

SILVA: [*Cutting in*] I run through fire to git that can, and I mean to keep it. [*Then to* ROCK]
Lock it up in the pick-up truck.

[ROCK *leaves. Unobtrusively some men follow him.*]

MARSHAL: Vacarro. Come over here. I want to have a word with you in one of these booths....

35]

ROCK.

[*He enters the men's room. As he approaches the urinal, the light is switched out and the door is thrown open at the same moment. Hoarse muffled shouts and sounds of struggle and a metallic clatter. Then the light goes on and* ROCK *is lying on the filthy cement floor, dazed.* VACARRO *enters. He goes to* ROCK.]

ROCK: They got the can, boss.

SILVA: Whose initials was on it? Huh? You said you seen some initials on the can.

ROCK: Naw. It just said – Sears and Roebuck.

[*The* MARSHAL *has come in and now reaches down and helps* ROCK *to regain his feet....*]

MARSHAL: Sears and Roebuck! That does it! Hahaha. Boy, git up and git some black coffee in yuh.

[*They pass through the door.*]

36]

THE MAIN ROOM.

MARSHAL: Ruby, Ruby! Give this boy some black coffee. He had a bad fall in the outhouse. Hawhawhaw....

[*But* SILVA *has steered* ROCK *out the front door and they are gone. The* MARSHAL *follows ...*]

37]

OUTSIDE.

[SILVA *and* ROCK *head towards the pick-up. The* MARSHAL appears in the doorway.]

MARSHAL: Vacarro!

[SILVA *and* ROCK *are at the truck. They wait for the* MARSHAL, *who is walking towards them.*]

MARSHAL: [*Soberly, plainly*] You take the advice of an old man who knows this county like the back of his hand. It's true you made a lot of enemies here. You happen to be a man with foreign blood. That's a disadvantage in this county. A disadvantage at least to begin with. But you added stubbornness and suspicion and resentment.

[VACARRO *makes an indescribable sound.*]

MARSHAL: I still say, a warm, friendly attitude on your part could have overcome that quickly. Instead, you stood off from people, refused to fraternize with them. Why not drop that attitude now? If someone set fire to your gin – I say that's not impossible. Also, I say we'll find him. But I don't have to tell you that if you now take your cotton across the river, or into another county, it will give rise to a lot of unfriendly speculation. No one would like it. No one.

[*Abruptly he turns and goes.*

ROCK *and* SILVA *are left alone. Men watch them from the surrounding cars . . . from the doorway.*]

SILVA: Did you ever see so many happy faces? Which one did it, Rock, you said you knew . . .?

ROCK: Well, they're all here . . . all here except one. The one that ain't here, I figure he did it. . . .

[*They're getting into the pick-up.*]

SILVA: Well, he's the one that's gonna gin out my cotton . . . .

[*The motor starts . . . the car goes into gear . . . and moves.*]

DISSOLVE.

38]

THE ROAD BEFORE ARCHIE LEE'S HOUSE.
THE NEXT MORNING.

[SILVA's *pick-up truck is leading a long line of cotton wagons — full of cotton.*]

39]

CLOSER SHOT. THE PICK-UP.
[*It stops.*]

40]

CLOSE ANGLE. SILVA AND ROCK.

ROCK: Maybe it figures. But it sure puzzles me why you want to bring your cotton to the guy that burned down your gin....

SILVA: You don't know the Christian proverbs about how you turn the other cheek when one has been slapped....

ROCK: When both cheeks has been kicked, what are you gonna turn then?

SILVA: You just got to turn and keep turning. Stop the wagons! I'm gonna drive up to his house.

[ROCK *hops out of the pick-up truck.*]

41]

OUTSIDE MEIGHAN HOUSE.
[*At an upstairs window we can just see* ARCHIE's *face. He is watching the wagons. Suddenly, he withdraws his head.*]

42]

UPSTAIRS. ARCHIE LEE MEIGHAN'S HOUSE.
[*He goes into a crazy, but silent Indian war dance. Then suddenly he can no longer contain himself and runs into ...*

43]

THE NURSERY
[*Enter* ARCHIE LEE.

BABY DOLL *is asleep in the crib. Her thumb is in her mouth.*
Like a child, she's trying to hold on to her sleep.
ARCHIE LEE *just whoops and hollers.* 'Baby Doll! Baby
Doll!', *etc.* 'Get up . . .' *etc.*
She can hardly believe her eyes. . . .
From downstairs the pick-up's horn sounds urgently.
AUNT ROSE COMFORT *rushes in breathlessly . . .*]

AUNT ROSE: Archie Lee, honesy. . . .

ARCHIE: [*Very Big Shot*] Get her up! Get her up, get her
washed and dressed and looking decent. Then bring her
down. The furniture is coming back today. . . .

[*He exits. . . .*]

44/65]

FRONT YARD.

[SILVA *and* ROCK *are sitting there in the pick-up truck. They
sit a little formally and stiffly and wait for* MEIGHAN, *who
comes barrelling out of the house, and up to the pick-up.*]

ARCHIE: Don't say a word. A little bird already told me that
you'd be bringing those twenty-seven wagons full of cotton
straight to my door, and I want you to know that you're a
very lucky fellow.

ROCK: [*Dryly*] How come?

ARCHIE: I mean that I am in a position to hold back other
orders and give you a priority. Well! Come on out of that
truck and have some coffee.

SILVA: What's your price?

ARCHIE: You remember my price. It hasn't changed.

[*Silence. The sense that* SILVA *is inspecting him.*]

ARCHIE: Hey, now looka here. Like you take shirts to a
laundry. You take them Friday and you want them Satur-
day. That's special. You got to pay special.

SILVA: How about your equipment? Hasn't changed either?

ARCHIE: A-1 shape! Always was! You ought to remember.

SILVA: I remember you needed a new saw-cylinder. You got
one?

ARCHIE: Can't find one on the market to equal the old one yet. Come on down and have a cup of coffee. We're all ready for you.

SILVA: I guess when you saw my gin burning down last night you must've suspected that you might get a good deal of business thrown your way in the morning.

ARCHIE: You want to know something?

SILVA: I'm always glad to know something when there's something to know.

[ROCK *laughs wildly.*]

ARCHIE: I never seen that fire of yours last night! Now come on over to my house and have some coffee.

[*The men get out of the truck.* ARCHIE *speaks to* ROCK.]

ARCHIE: You come too, if you want to. . . . No, sir, I never seen that fire of yours last night. We hit the sack right after supper and didn't know until breakfast time this morning that your cotton gin had burned down.

[*They go up on the porch.*]

Yes sir, it's providential. That's the only word for it. Hey, Baby Doll! It's downright providential. Baby Doll! Come out here, Baby Doll!

[*Enter* BABY DOLL.]

You come right over here and meet Mr Vacarro from the Syndicate Plantation.

BABY DOLL: Oh hello. Has something gone wrong, Archie Lee?

ARCHIE: What do you mean, Baby Doll?

BABY DOLL: I just thought that maybe something went —

ARCHIE: What is your first name, Vacarro?

SILVA: Silva.

ARCHIE: How do you spell it?

[SILVA *spells it.* 'Capital S-I-L-V-A.' *Meantime, his eyes on* BABY DOLL.]

ARCHIE: Oh. Like a silver lining? Every cloud has got a silver lining.

BABY DOLL: What is that from? The Bible?

SILVA: No, the Mother Goose book.

BABY DOLL: That name sounds foreign.

SILVA: It is, Mrs Meighan. I'm known as the wop that runs the Syndicate Plantation.

[ARCHIE LEE *claps him heartily on the back.* SILVA *stiffly withdraws from the contact.*]

ARCHIE: Don't call yourself names. Let other folks call you names! Well, you're a lucky little fellow, silver, gold, or even nickel-plated, you sure are lucky that I can take a job of this size right now. It means some cancellations, but you're my closest neighbour. I believe in the good-neighbour policy, Mr Vacarro. You do me a good turn and I'll do you a good turn. Tit for tat. Tat for tit is the policy we live on. *Aunt Rose Comfort!* Baby Doll, git your daddy's ole maid sister to break out a fresh pot of coffee for Mr Vacarro.

BABY DOLL: You get her.

ARCHIE: And honey, I want you to entertain this gentleman. Ha! Ha! Look at her blush. Haha! This is my baby. This is my little girl, every precious ounce of her is mine, all mine.

[*He exits – crazily elated, calling 'Aunt Rose'.*

CUT BACK to BABY DOLL. *She emits an enormous yawn.*]

BABY DOLL: Excuse my yawn. We went to bed kinda late last night.

CUT TO SILVA. He notices the discrepancy. He looks at ROCK, *who also noticed.*

As if she were talking of a title of great distinction.]

So. You're a wop?

SILVA: [*With ironic politeness*] I'm a Sicilian, Mrs Meighan. A very ancient people. . . .

BABY DOLL: [*Trying out the word*] Sish! Sish!

SILVA: No, ma'am. Siss! Sicilian.

BABY DOLL: Oh, how unusual.

[ARCHIE LEE *bursts back out on the porch.*]

ARCHIE: And honey, at noon, take Mr Vacarro in town to the Kotton King Hotel for a chicken dinner. Sign my name! It's only when bad luck hits you, Mr Vacarro, that you find out who your friends are. I mean to prove it. All right. Let's get GOING! Baby, knock me a kiss!

BABY DOLL: What's the matter with you? Have you got drunk before breakfast?

ARCHIE: Hahaha.

BABY DOLL: Somebody say something funny?

ARCHIE: Offer this young fellow here to a cup of coffee. I got to get busy ginning that cotton. [*He extends his great sweaty hand to* VACARRO.] Glad to be able to help you out of this bad situation. It's the good-neighbour policy.

SILVA: What is?

ARCHIE: You do me a good turn and I'll do you a good turn some time in the future.

SILVA: I see.

ARCHIE: Tit for tat, tat for tit, as they say. Hahaha! Well, make yourself at home here. Baby Doll, I want you to make this gentleman comfortable in the house.

BABY DOLL: You can't make anyone comfortable in this house. Lucky if you can find a chair to sit in.

[*But* MEIGHAN *is gone, calling out, 'Move those wagons', etc., etc.*]

BABY DOLL: [*After a slight pause*] Want some coffee?

SILVA: No. Just a cool drink of water, thank you, ma'am.

BABY DOLL: The kitchen water runs warm, but if you got the energy to handle an old-fashioned pump, you can get you a real cool drink from that there cistern at the side of the house. . . .

SILVA: I got energy to burn.

[VACARRO *strides through the tall seeding grass to an old cistern with a hand pump, deep in the side yard.* ROCK *follows.* OLD FUSSY *goes 'Squawk, Squawk', and* AUNT ROSE COMFORT *is singing 'Rock of Ages' in the kitchen.*]

SILVA: [*Looking about contemptuously as he crosses to the cistern*] Dump their garbage in the yard, phew! *Ignorance* and *Indulgence* and *stink*!

ROCK: I thought that young Mizz Meighan smelt pretty good.

SILVA: You keep your nose with the cotton. And hold that dipper, I'll pump.

AUNT ROSE: Sometimes water comes and sometimes it don't.

[*The water comes pouring from the rusty spout.*]

SILVA: This time it did. . . .

BABY DOLL: Bring me a dipper of that nice cool well water, please.

[ROCK *crosses immediately with the filled dipper.*]

SILVA: Hey!

OLD FUSSY: Squawk, squawk!!

AUNT ROSE: I don't have the strength any more in my arm that I used to, to draw water out of that pump.

[*She approaches, smoothing her ancient apron.* VACARRO *is touched by her aged grace.*]

SILVA: Would you care for a drink?

AUNT ROSE: How do you do? I'm Aunt Rose Comfort McCorkle. My brother was Baby Doll's daddy, Mr T. C. Carson. I've been visiting here since . . . since . . . [*She knits her ancient brow, unable to recall precisely when the long visit started.*]

SILVA: I hope you don't mind drinking out of a gourd.

[*He hands her the gourd of well water.* ROCK *returns, saying aloud . . .*

ROCK: I could think of worse ways to spend a hot afternoon than delivering cool well water to Mrs Meighan.

AUNT ROSE: SCUSE ME PLEASE! That ole hen, Fussy, has just gone back in my kitchen!

[*She runs crazily to the house.* BABY DOLL *has wandered back to the cistern as if unconsciously drawn by the magnetism of the two young males.*]

BABY DOLL: They's such a difference in water! You wouldn't think so, but there certainly is.

SILVA: [*To* ROCK] Hold the dipper, I'll pump!

[*He brings up more water; then strips off his shirt and empties the brimming dipper over his head and at the same time he says to* ROCK . . .]

SILVA: Go stay with the cotton. Go on! Stay with the cotton.

[ROCK *goes.*]

BABY DOLL: I wouldn't dare to expose myself like that. I take such terrible sunburn.

SILVA: I like the feel of a hot sun on my body.

BABY DOLL: That's not sunburn though. You're natcherally dark.

SILVA: Yes. Don't you have garbage collectors on Tiger Tail Road?

BABY DOLL: It cost a little bit extra to git them to come out here and Archie Lee Meighan claimed it was highway robbery! Refused to pay! Now the place is swarming with flies an' mosquitoes and – oh, I don't know, I almost give up sometimes.

SILVA: And did I understand you to say that you've got a bunch of unfurnished rooms in the house?

BABY DOLL: Five complete sets of furniture hauled away! By the Ideal Pay As You Go Plan Furniture Company.

SILVA: When did this misfortune – fall upon you?

BABY DOLL: Why, yestiddy! Ain't that awful?

SILVA: Both of us had misfortunes on the same day.

BABY DOLL: Huh?

SILVA: You lost your furniture. My cotton gin burned down.

BABY DOLL: [*Not quite with it*] Oh.

SILVA: Quite a coincidence!

BABY DOLL: Huh?

SILVA: I said it was a coincidence of misfortune.

BABY DOLL: Well, sure – after all what can you do with a bunch of unfurnished rooms.

SILVA: Well, you could play hide-and-seek.

BABY DOLL: Not me. I'm not athletic.

SILVA: I take it you've not had this place long, Mrs Meighan.

BABY DOLL: No, we ain't had it long.

SILVA: When I arrived in this county to take over the management of the Syndicate Plantation ... [*Chops at grass with crop*] this place was empty. I was told it was haunted. Then you all moved in.

BABY DOLL: Yes it was haunted, and that's why Archie Lee bought it for almost nothing. [*She pauses in the sun as if dazed*] Sometimes I don't know where to go, what to do.

SILVA: That's not uncommon. People enter this world without instruction.

BABY DOLL: [*She's lost him again*] Huh?

SILVA: I said people come into this world without instructions of where to go, what to do, so they wander a little and ...

[AUNT ROSE *sings rather sweetly from the kitchen, wind blows an Aeolian refrain.*]

then go away....

[*Now* BABY DOLL *gives him a quick look, almost perceptive and then ...*]

BABY DOLL: Yah, well ...

SILVA: *Drift* – for a while and then ... *vanish.* [*He stoops to pick a dandelion*] And so make room for newcomers! Old goers, newcomers! Back and forth, going and coming, rush, rush!! *Permanent? Nothing!* [*Blows on the seeding dandelion*] Anything living! ... last long enough to take it serious.

[*They are walking together. There is the beginning of some weird understanding between them.*

They have stopped strolling by a poetic wheelless chassis of an old Pierce-Arrow limousine in the side yard.]

BABY DOLL: This is the old Pierce-Arrow car that belonged to the lady that used to own this place and haunts it now.

[VACARRO *steps gravely forward and opens the back door for her.*]

SILVA: Where to, madam?

BABY DOLL: Oh, you're playing *show-fer!* It's a good place to sit when the house isn't furnished....

[*She enters and sinks on the ruptured upholstery. He gravely puts the remnant of the dandelion in the cone-shaped cut-glass vase in a bracket by the back seat of the old limousine.*]

BABY DOLL: [*Laughing with sudden, childish laughter*] Drive me along the river as fast as you can with all the windows open to cool me off.

SILVA: Fine, madam!

BABY DOLL: [*Suddenly aware of his body near her*] Showfers sit in the front seat.

SILVA: Front seat's got no cushion.

BABY DOLL: It's hard to find a place to sit around here since the Ideal Pay As You Go Plan people lost patience. To sit in comfort, I mean. . . .

SILVA: It's hard to sit in comfort when the Ideal Pay As You Go Plan people lose their patience and your gin burns down.

BABY DOLL: Oh! But . . .

SILVA: Huh?

BABY DOLL: You said that like you thought there was . . .

SILVA: What?

BABY DOLL: Some connexion! Excuse me, I want to get out and I can't get over your legs. . . .

[*Her apathy is visited by a sudden inexplicable flurry of panic. He has his boots propped against the back of the front seat.*]

SILVA: You can't get over my legs?

BABY DOLL: No. I'm not athletic.

[*She tries to open door on other side, but it is blocked by the trunk of a pecan tree.*]

SILVA: But it's cool here and comfortable to sit in. What's this here??

[*He has seized her wrist on which hangs a bracelet of many little gold charms. She sinks somewhat uneasily in beside him.*]

BABY DOLL: It's a, it's a . . . charm bracelet.

[*He begins to finger the many little gold charms attached.*]

BABY DOLL: My daddy gave it to me. Them there's the ten commandments.

SILVA: And these?

BABY DOLL: My birthdays. It's stretchable. One for each birthday.

SILVA: How many charming birthdays have you had?

BABY DOLL: As many as I got charms hanging on that bracelet.

SILVA: Mind if I count 'em? [*They are close.*] Fourteen, fifteen, sixteen, seventeen, eighteen, nineteen, and . . .

BABY DOLL: That's all. I'll be twenty tomorrow. Tomorrow is Election Day and Election Day is my birthday. I was born on the day that Frank Delano Roosevelt was elected for his first term.

SILVA: A great day for the country for both reasons.

BABY DOLL: He was a man to respect.

SILVA: And you're a lady to respect, Mrs Meighan.

BABY DOLL: [*Sadly and rather touchingly*] Me? Oh, no – I never got past the fourth grade.

SILVA: Why'd you quit?

BABY DOLL: I had a great deal of trouble with long division. . . .

SILVA: Yeah?

BABY DOLL: The teacher would tell me to go to the blackboard and work out a problem in long division and I would go to the blackboard and lean my head against it and cry and cry and – cry. . . .
Whew! I think the porch would be cooler. Mr Vacarro, I can't get over your legs.

SILVA: You want to move my legs.

BABY DOLL: Yes, otherwise I can't get out of the car. . . .

SILVA: Okay.

[*He raises his legs so she can get out. Which she does, and continues . . .*]

BABY DOLL: YES, I would cry and cry. . . . Well . . . soon after that I left school. A girl without education is – without education. . . . Whew. . . . Feel kind of dizzy. Hope I'm not gettin' a *sun* stroke. – I better sit in the shade. . . .

[VACARRO *follows her casually into the shade of the pecan tree where there's a decrepit old swing. Suddenly, he leaps into branches and then down with a pecan. He cracks it in his mouth and hands her the kernels. . . .*]

BABY DOLL: Mr Vacarro! I wouldn't dream! – excuse me, but I just wouldn't dream! of eating a nut that a man had cracked in his mouth. . . .

SILVA: You've got many refinements. I don't think you need to worry about your failure at long division. I mean, after all, you got through short division, and short division is all that a lady ought to be called on to cope with. . . .

BABY DOLL: Well, I – ought to go in, but I get depressed when I pass through those empty rooms. . . .

SILVA: All the rooms empty?

BABY DOLL: All but the nursery. And the kitchen. The stuff in those rooms was paid for. . .

SILVA: You have a child in the nursery?

BABY DOLL: Me? No. I sleep in the nursery myself. Let down the slats on the crib. . . .

SILVA: Why do you sleep in the nursery?

BABY DOLL: Mr Vacarro, that's a *personal* question.

[*There is a pause.*]

BABY DOLL: I ought to go in . . . but . . . you know there are places in that house which I never been in. I mean the attic for instance. Most of the time I'm afraid to go into that house by myself. Last night when the fire broke out I sat here on this swing for hours and hours till Archie Lee got home, because I was scared to enter this old place by myself.

[VACARRO *has caught this discrepancy too.*]

SILVA: It musta been scary here without your husband to look after you.

BABY DOLL: I'm tellin' you! The fire lit up the whole countryside and it made big crazy shadows and we didn't have a coke in the house and the heat and the mosquitoes and – I was mad at Archie Lee.

SILVA: Mad at Mr Meighan? What about?

BABY DOLL: Oh, he went off and left me settin' here without a coke in the place.

SILVA: Went off and left you, did he??!!

BABY DOLL: Well, he certainly did. Right after supper and when he got back, the fire'd already broke out. I got smoke in my eyes and my nose and throat. I was in such a wornout nervous condition it made me cry. Finally I took two teaspoons of paregoric.

SILVA: Sounds like you passed a very uncomfortable night.

BABY DOLL: Sounds like? Well it was!

SILVA: So Mr Meighan – you say – disappeared after supper.

BABY DOLL: [*After a pause*] Huh?

SILVA: You say Mr Meighan left the house for a while after supper?

[*Something in his tone makes her aware that she has spoken indiscreetly.*]

BABY DOLL: Oh – uh – just for a moment.

SILVA: Just for a moment, huh? How long a moment?

BABY DOLL: What are you driving at, Mr Vacarro?

SILVA: Driving at? Nothing.

BABY DOLL: You're looking at me so funny.

SILVA: How long a moment did he disappear for? Can you remember, Mrs Meighan?

BABY DOLL: What difference does that make? What's it to you, anyhow?

SILVA: Why should you mind my asking?

BABY DOLL: You make this sound like I was on trial for something.

SILVA: Don't you like to pretend like you're a witness?

BABY DOLL: Witness of what, Mr Vacarro?

SILVA: Why – for instance – say – a case of arson!

BABY DOLL: Case of –? What is – arson?

SILVA: The wilful destruction of property by fire. [*Slaps his boots sharply with the riding crop*]

BABY DOLL: Oh! [*She nervously fingers her purse*]

SILVA: There's one thing I always notice about you ladies.

BABY DOLL: What's that?

SILVA: Whenever you get nervous, you always like to have something in your hands to hold on to – like that big white purse.

BABY DOLL: This purse?

SILVA: Yes, it gives you something to hold on to, isn't that right?

BABY DOLL: Well, I do always like to have something in my hands.

SILVA: Sure you do. You feel what a lot of uncertain things there are. Gins burn down. No one know how or why. Volunteer fire departments don't have decent equipment. They're no protection. The afternoon sun is too hot. The trees! They're no protection! The house – it's haunted! It's no protection. Your husband. He's across the road and busy. He's no protection! The goods that dress is made of – it's light and thin – it's no protection. So what do you do, Mrs Meighan? You pick up that white kid purse. It's something to hold on to.

46

BABY DOLL: Now, Mr Silva. Don't you go and be getting any – funny ideas.

SILVA: Ideas about what?

BABY DOLL: My husband disappearing – after supper. I can explain that.

SILVA: Can you?

BABY DOLL: Sure I can.

SILVA: Good! How do you explain it? [*He stares at her. She looks down*] What's the matter? Can't you collect your thoughts, Mrs Meighan?

[*Pause*]

Your mind's a blank on the subject??

BABY DOLL: Look here, now. . . .

SILVA: You find it impossible to remember just what your husband disappeared for after supper? You can't imagine what kind of an errand he went out on, can you?

BABY DOLL: No! No! I can't!

SILVA: But when he returned – let's see – the fire had just broken out at the Syndicate Plantation.

BABY DOLL: Mr Vacarro, I don't have the slightest idea what you could be driving at.

SILVA: You're a very unsatisfactory witness, Mrs Meighan.

BABY DOLL: I never can think when people – stare straight at me.

SILVA: Okay, I'll look away then. [*Turns his back to her*] Now, does that improve your memory any? Now are you able to concentrate on the question?

BABY DOLL: Huh?

SILVA: No? You're not? [*Grins evilly*] Well – should we drop the subject??

BABY DOLL: Sure do wish you would!

SILVA: Sure, there's no use crying over a burnt-down gin. And besides, like your husband says – this world is built on the principle of tit for tat.

BABY DOLL: What do you mean?

SILVA: Nothing at all specific. Mind if I . . .?

BABY DOLL: What?

[SILVA *approaches the swing where she sits.*]

SILVA: You want to move over a little and make some room?

BABY DOLL: [*Shifts slightly*] Is that room enough for you?

SILVA: Enough for me. How about you?

BABY DOLL: Is it strong enough to support us both?

SILVA: I hope. Let's swing a little. You seem all tense. Motion relaxes people. It's like a cradle. A cradle relaxes a baby. They call you 'Baby', don't they?

BABY DOLL: That's sort of a pet name.

SILVA: Well in the swing you can relax like a cradle. . . .

BABY DOLL: Not if you swing it so high. It shakes me up.

SILVA: Well, I'll swing it low then. Are you relaxed?

BABY DOLL: I'm relaxed enough. As much as necessary.

SILVA: No, you're not. Your nerves are tied up.

BABY DOLL: You make me nervous.

SILVA: Just swinging with you?

BABY DOLL: Not just that.

SILVA: What else then?

BABY DOLL: All them questions you asked me about the fire.

SILVA: I only inquired about your husband – about his leaving the house after supper.

BABY DOLL: Why should I have to explain why he left the house? Besides, I did. I think I explained that to you.

SILVA: You said that he left the house before the fire broke out.

BABY DOLL: What about it?

SILVA: Why did he leave the house?

BABY DOLL: I explained that to you. I explained that to you.

SILVA: What was the explanation? I forgot it.

[BABY DOLL'*s face is beaded with sweat. To save her life she can't think, can't think at all.*]

BABY DOLL: [*Just to gain a moment*] Oh, you're talking about my husband?

SILVA: That's who I'm talking about.

BABY DOLL: How should I know!!!

SILVA: You mean where he went after supper.

BABY DOLL: Yes!! How should I know where he went.

SILVA: I thought you said you explained that to me.

BABY DOLL: I did! I explained it to you!

SILVA: Well, if you don't know, how could you explain it to me?

BABY DOLL: [*Turning*] There's no reason why I should explain things to you.

SILVA: Then just relax.

[*They swing.*]

As I was saying, that was a lovely remark your husband made.

BABY DOLL: What remark did he make?

SILVA: The good-neighbour policy. I see what he means by that now.

BABY DOLL: He was talking about the President's speech.

SILVA: I think he was talking about something closer to home. *You do me* a good turn and *I'll do you* one. That was the way he put it. [*Delicately he removes a little piece of lint from her arm.*]

SILVA: There now!

BABY DOLL: [*Nervously*] Thanks.

SILVA: There's a lot of fine cotton lint floating around in the air.

BABY DOLL: I know there is. It irritates my sinus.

SILVA: Well, you're a delicate woman.

BABY DOLL: Delicate? Me? Oh no. I'm a good-size woman.

SILVA: There's a lot of you, but every bit of you is delicate. Choice. Delectable, I might say.

BABY DOLL: Huh?

SILVA: [*Running his finger lightly over her skin*] You're fine fibred. And smooth. And soft.

BABY DOLL: Our conversation is certainly taking a personal turn!

SILVA: Yes! You make me think of cotton. [*Still caressing her arm another moment*] No! No fabric, no kind of cloth, not even satin or silk cloth, or no kind of fibre, not even cotton fibre has the ab-so-lute delicacy of your skin!

BABY DOLL: Well! Should I say thanks or something?

SILVA: No, just smile, Mrs Meighan. You have an attractive smile. Dimples!!

BABY DOLL: No ...

SILVA: Yes, you have! Smile, Mrs Meighan! Come on! Smile!
   [BABY DOLL *averts her face, smiles helplessly.*]
   There now. See? You've got them! [*Delicately, he touches one of the indentations in her cheek.*]

BABY DOLL: Please don't touch me. I don't like to be touched.

SILVA: Then why do you giggle?

BABY DOLL: Can't help it. You make me feel kind of hysterical, Mr Vacarro ... Mr Vacarro ...

SILVA: Yes?

BABY DOLL: [*A different attack, more feminine, pleading*] I hope you don't think that Archie Lee was mixed up in that fire. I swear to goodness he never left the front porch. I remember it perfectly now. We just set here on the swing till the fire broke out and then we drove into town.

SILVA: To celebrate!

BABY DOLL: No, no, no!

SILVA: Twenty-seven wagons full of cotton's a pretty big piece of business to fall into your lap like a gift from the gods, Mrs Meighan.

BABY DOLL: I thought you said we would drop the subject.

SILVA: You brought it up that time.

BABY DOLL: Well, please don't try to mix me up any more, I swear to goodness the fire had already broke out when he got back.

SILVA: That's not what you told me a moment ago.

BABY DOLL: You got me all twisted up. We went in town. The fire broke out and we didn't know about it.

SILVA: I thought you said it irritated your sinus.

BABY DOLL: Oh my God, you sure put words in my mouth. Maybe I'd better make us some lemonade.
   [*She starts to get up. Silva pulls her down.*]
   What did you do that for?

SILVA: I don't want to be deprived of your company yet. [*He lightly switches her legs with his crop.*]

BABY DOLL: [*Twisting*] Mr Vacarro, you're getting awfully familiar.

SILVA: Haven't you got any fun-loving spirit about you?

BABY DOLL: This isn't fun.

SILVA: Then why do you giggle?

BABY DOLL: I'm ticklish!

SILVA: Ticklish!

BABY DOLL: Yes, quit switching me, will you?

SILVA: I'm just shooing the flies off.

BABY DOLL: They don't hurt nothing. And would you mind moving your arm?

SILVA: Don't be so skittish!

BABY DOLL: All right! I'll get up then.

SILVA: Go on.

BABY DOLL: [*Trying*] I feel so weak. [*She pulls herself away from him*] Oh! My head's so buzzy.

SILVA: Fuzzy?

BABY DOLL: Fuzzy and buzzy. My head's swinging around. It's that swinging.... Is something on my arm?

SILVA: No.

BABY DOLL: Then what are you brushing?

SILVA: Sweat off. Let me wipe it.... [*He brushes her arm with his handkerchief.*]

BABY DOLL: [*Laughing weakly*] No, please don't. It feels funny.

SILVA: How does it feel?

BABY DOLL: Funny! All up and down. You cut it out now. If you don't cut it out I'm going to call.

SILVA: Call who?

BABY DOLL: That nigger who's cuttin' the grass across the road.

SILVA: Go on. Call then.

BABY DOLL: Hey! [*Her voice is faint, weak*] Hey, boy, boy!

SILVA: Can't you call any louder?

BABY DOLL: I feel so funny! What's the matter with me?

SILVA: You're just relaxing. You're big. There's a lot of you and it's all relaxing. So give in. Stop getting yourself all excited.

BABY DOLL: I'm not – but you....

SILVA: I!???

BABY DOLL: Yes. You. Suspicions. The ideas you have about my husband ... suspicions.

SILVA: Suspicions? Such as ...

BABY DOLL: Such as he burnt your gin down.

SILVA: Well?

BABY DOLL: He didn't.

SILVA: Didn't he?

BABY DOLL: I'm going inside. I'm going in the house.
  [*She starts in. He follows close beside her.*]

SILVA: But you're afraid of the house! Do you believe in
  ghosts, Mrs Meighan? I do. I believe in the presence of evil
  spirits.

BABY DOLL: What evil spirits you talking about now?

SILVA: Spirits of violence – and cunning – malevolence –
  cruelty – treachery – destruction....

BABY DOLL: Oh, them's just human characteristics.

SILVA: They're evil spirits that haunt the human heart and
  take possession of it, and spread from one human heart to
  another human heart the way that a fire goes springing
  from leaf to leaf and branch to branch in a tree till a forest
  is all aflame with it – the birds take flight – the wild things
  are suffocated ... everything green and beautiful is des-
  troyed....

BABY DOLL: You have got fire on the brain.

SILVA: I see it as more than it seems to be on the surface. I
  saw it last night as an explosion of those evil spirits that
  haunt the human heart – I fought it! I ran into it, beating it,
  stamping it, shouting the curse of God at it! They dragged
  me out, suffocating. I was defeated! When I came to, lying
  on the ground – the fire had won the battle, and all around
  was a ring of human figures! The fire lit their faces! I looked
  up. And they were illuminated! Their eyes, their teeth were
  SHINING!! SEE! LIKE THIS! [*He twists his face into a
  grotesque grimace of pleasure. He holds her. They have arrived at
  the door to the interior of the house.*] Yeah! Like this! Like
  this!! [*He thrusts his grimacing face at her. She springs back,
  frightened.*]

BABY DOLL: Hey! Please! Don't do that! Don't scare me!

SILVA: The faces I saw – were grinning! Then I knew! I knew
  the fire was not accidental! [*He holds her fast at the door.*]

BABY DOLL: [*Weakly*] Not accidental?

SILVA: No, it was not accidental! It was an expression, a manifestation of the human will to *destroy*.

BABY DOLL: I wouldn't – feel that way – about it. . . .

SILVA: I do! I do! And so I say I believe in ghosts, in haunted places, places haunted by the people that occupy them with hearts overrun by demons of hate and destruction. I believe this place, this house is haunted. . . . What's the matter?

BABY DOLL: [*Now thoroughly shaken*] I don't know. . . .

SILVA: You're scared to enter the house, is that the trouble?

BABY DOLL: [*Calling*] Aunt Rose. Aunt Rose!! [*No answer*] That old woman can't hear a thing.

SILVA: There's no question about it. This place is haunted.

BABY DOLL: I'm getting – I'm getting so thirsty, so hot and thirsty!

SILVA: Then why don't you treat yourself to a drink of cold water?

BABY DOLL: I – I thought I might make us a – pitcher of – cold lemonade.

[*For some reason, BABY DOLL doesn't want to enter the front door and she starts around the porch away from him. A board cracks under her weight. She screams, staggers. SILVA rushes to her and seizes her plump arm, placing an arm behind her. She giggles weakly, but for the first time accepting his help.*]

BABY DOLL: The place is – collapsing right underneath me!

SILVA: You're trembling, Mrs Meighan, shaking all over!

BABY DOLL: Your – your hands are so – hot – I don't think I ever felt hands as hot as your hands, they're – why they're like a couple of plates – took right out of – the oven!

SILVA: Burn, do they?

BABY DOLL: Yeah, they – *do*, they *burn* – me. . . .

SILVA: The idea of lemonade is very attractive. I would be glad to help you squeeze the lemons. [*Tightens the pressure of his hands.*]

BABY DOLL: I know you would! I mean I – thanks, but – I can do it myself.

SILVA: You don't want my assistance, Mrs Meighan?

BABY DOLL: Naw, it ain't necessary. . . .

SILVA: But then you would have to go into the house alone and the house is haunted! I better go in with you!

BABY DOLL: . . . No, it ain't necessary! [*She is panting.*]

SILVA: You want me to stay on the porch?

BABY DOLL: Yeh, you stay on the porch!

SILVA: Why *shouldn't* I come inside?

BABY DOLL: No reason, just – just . . .! [*She giggles weakly*] You stay out here while I make the lemonade and . . .

SILVA: All right. Go on, Mrs Meighan. . . .

BABY DOLL: You stay out here. . . .

[*He doesn't answer. She stares at him, not moving.*]

SILVA: Now what's the matter now? Why don't you go in?

BABY DOLL: I don't think I better. I think I will go across the road to the gin. They got a water cooler. . . .

SILVA: The water cooler's for coloured. A lady, a white lady like you, the wife of the big white boss, would place herself in an undignified position if she went over the road to drink with the hands! They might get notions about her! Unwholesome ideas! The sight of her soft white flesh, so smooth and abundant, might inflame their – natures . . .

[*Suddenly* BABY DOLL *sees something off and . . .*]

66]

NEGRO BOY COMING DOWN THE ROAD.

[*He pushes a lawnmower. Behind him can be seen* ARCHIE LEE's *gin, working.*]

67]

BABY DOLL.

[*She rushes past* SILVA *in the direction of the Negro boy, runs unsteadily as if she were drunk, across the unkempt lawn and out into the shimmering brilliance of the road.*]

BABY DOLL: Boy! Boy! I want you to cut my grass.

BOY: Can't now, ma'am.

BABY DOLL: Yes, you can.

BOY: I got a job cuttin' grass across Tiger Tail Bayou.

BABY DOLL: You cut grass here. [*Her intensity frightens the boy.*]

BOY: Yes, ma'am, later.

BABY DOLL: NO! NOW! RIGHT NOW! I – I'll pay you five dollars. . . .

BOY: Yes, ma'am.

BABY DOLL: I'll pay you five dollars . . . but *now*.

BOY: [*Scared to death*] Yes, ma'am. Yes, ma'am.

BABY DOLL: And work close to the house. Hear! Speak up. Do you hear . . .?

BOY: Yes, ma'am. Yes, ma'am.

[BABY DOLL *sees* . . .]

68]

SILVA.

[*As he comes into the picture, she retreats, walking backwards. Then there is a hoot from the gin. The sound from the gin suddenly stops. This calls her attention to the gin and she starts in that direction.*]

SILVA: Boy.

BOY: Yes, sir.

SILVA: Here's that five dollars the lady was mentioning.

BOY: Yes, sir.

SILVA: Only she don't want you to cut the grass.

BOY: Yes, sir.

SILVA: So you go on like you were. Understand?

BOY: Oh, yes, sir. Thank you, sir. [*The boy, now completely bewildered, goes on, as he was.*]

69]

INTERIOR. COTTON GIN.

[*Something is wrong. The men, including* ROCK, *are gathered around a large piece of machinery. There is the characteristic debate as to what is wrong, opinions differing.*

Onto to this rather hectic group runs BABY DOLL. ARCHIE *turns on her viciously.*]

ARCHIE: What're you doin' here, have you gone crazy??

BABY DOLL: I want to tell you something! You big slob.
[*This is just a little more than a desperate and harassed* ARCHIE *can bear. He suddenly comes across and smacks* BABY DOLL. *Good and hard.*]

ARCHIE: I told you never, never, never, to cross that road to this cotton gin –

70]

CLOSE SHOT. SILVA.
[*He has entered and seen the action.*]

71]

ARCHIE.
[*He notices* SILVA.]
ARCHIE: . . . this cotton gin when niggers are working here.
BABY DOLL: You left me . . . you know what you left with me over there. . . .
[ARCHIE'*s eye wanders over to* SILVA, *and* BABY DOLL *sees him and clams up.*]

72]

SILVA.
[*He now officially enters the scene.*]
SILVA: How's progress, Mr Meighan?
ARCHIE Fine! Great!
SILVA: Personally, I can't hear the gin at all.
BABY DOLL: [*Full of disgust*] Big Shot! [*And she exits.*]
SILVA: What's holding up?
ARCHIE: Nothing. . . .
SILVA: Rock!
[SILVA'*s own foreman steps forward.*]
ROCK: His saw-cylinder is busted.
SILVA: It figures. I inspected your equipment, Meighan, before I put in my own and I put up my own cotton gin because this equipment was rotten, was rotten, and still is rotten. Now it's quarterpast two by my watch

and I counted twenty-three fully loaded wagons still out on your runway. And if you can't move those wagons any faster ...

ARCHIE: Now don't go into any hysterics. You Italians are prone to get too excited. ...

SILVA: Never mind about we Italians. You better get yourself a new saw-cylinder and get this contraption running again. And if you can't get one in Clarksdale, you better go to Tunica, and if you can't get one in Tunica, you better go to Memphis, and if you can't get one in Memphis, keep going to St Louis. Now get on your horse.

ARCHIE: Now listen to me, Silva –

SILVA: One more crack out of you, I'm going to haul across the river. I said get on your horse.

[MEIGHAN *hesitates. Then decides he must swallow this humiliation. There's nothing else for him to do under the circumstances. He exits.*

SILVA *calls* ROCK *over close.*]

SILVA; [*Sotto voce*] I got a saw-cylinder in our commissary. Go get it and bring Hank over to help you put it in. Get this thing running. He ain't gonna get one in Clarksdale, and if he goes to Memphis – well, don't wait for him. [*And he exits.*]

73]

ARCHIE LEE IN HIS CHEVY.
[*He nearly runs* BABY DOLL *over.*]

BABY DOLL: Archie Lee! Archie Lee! Archie Lee! [*She stumbles to her knees. She's sobbing. She rests a moment in the tall grass.*]

74]

SILVA.
[*He runs up to her and stoops down to help her.*]

BABY DOLL: Le' me go. Le' me go. [*She gets up and moves away from him towards her house.*]

75]

AUNT ROSE COMFORT, AND BABY DOLL.

[AUNT ROSE *comes out of the house all dressed up.*]

BABY DOLL: Aunt Rose Comfort.

[AUNT ROSE COMFORT *rushes past her.*]

BABY DOLL: Aunt Rose Comfort!! Where are you going?

AUNT ROSE: I have to see a sick friend at the county hospital.

[*And she is gone.* SILVA *has caught up to* BABY DOLL *again.*]

BABY DOLL: You might as well shout at the moon as that old woman.

SILVA: You didn't want her to go??

BABY DOLL: She's got no business leaving me here alone.

SILVA: It makes you uneasy to be alone here with me.

BABY DOLL: I think she just pretended not to hear me. She has a passion for chocolate candy and she watches the newspapers like a hawk to see if anybody she knows is registered at the county hospital.

SILVA: Hospital ...?

BABY DOLL: They give candy to patients at the county hospital, friends and relations send them flowers and candy and Aunt Rose Comfort calls on them and eats up their chocolate candy. [SILVA *explodes with laughter.*]

BABY DOLL: One time an old lady friend of Aunt Rose Comfort was dying at the county hospital and Aunt Rose Comfort went over and ate up a two-pound box of chocolate cherries while the old lady was dying, finished it all, hahahaha, while the old lady was dying.

[*They're both laughing together.*]

I like ole people – they're crazy. . . .

[*They both laugh together. . . .*]

SILVA: Mrs Meighan. . . . May I ask you something? Of a personal nature?

BABY DOLL: What?

SILVA: Are you really married to Mr Meighan?

BABY DOLL: Mr Vacarro, that's a personal question.

SILVA: All questions are more or less personal, Mrs Meighan.

BABY DOLL: Well, when I married I wasn't ready for marriage.

I was still eighteen, but my daddy was practically on his death-bed and wanted to see me took care of before he died. Well, ole Archie Lee had been hanging around like a sick dog for quite some time and ... the boys are a sorry lot around here. Ask you to the movies and take you to the old rock quarry instead. You have to get out of the car and throw rocks at 'em, oh, I've had some experiences with boys that would curl your hair if I told you – some – experiences which I've had with boys!! But Archie Lee Meighan was an older fellow and in those days, well, his business was better. You hadn't put up that cotton gin of yours and Archie Lee was ginning out a lot of cotton. You remember?

SILVA: Yes, I remember. ...

BABY DOLL: Well, I told my daddy I wasn't ready for marriage and my daddy told Archie Lee that I wasn't ready for it and he promised my daddy he'd wait till I was ready.

SILVA: Then the marriage was postponed?

BABY DOLL: Not the wedding, no, we had the wedding, my daddy gave me away. ...

SILVA: But you said that Archie Lee waited?

BABY DOLL: Yes, *after* the wedding ... he waited.

SILVA: For what?

BABY DOLL: For me to be ready for marriage.

SILVA: How long did he have to wait?

BABY DOLL: Oh, he's still waiting! Of course, we had an agreement that ... well ... I mean I told him that I'd be ready on my twentieth birthday – I mean ready or *not*. ...

SILVA: And that's tomorrow?

BABY DOLL: Uh-huh.

SILVA: And are you ... will you – be ready?

BABY DOLL: That all depends.

SILVA: What on?

BABY DOLL: Whether or not the furniture comes back – I guess. ...

SILVA: Your husband sweats more than any man I know and now I understand why!!

[*There is a pause. They look at each other. Then* BABY DOLL *looks away. Then with a sudden access of energy she enters the house, slams the screen door in his face and latches it.*]

BABY DOLL: *There now! You wait here! You just wait out here!*

SILVA: [*Grinning at the screen door*] Yes, ma'am. I will wait.

76]

INTERIOR. DIMLY LIT ENTRANCE HALL OF MEIGHAN HOUSE.

[BABY DOLL *turns from screen door to porch and stumbles along the vast and shadowy hall towards the dim light of the kitchen. As soon as she disappears,* VACARRO *is seen through screen door. He jerks out a pocket-knife and rips a hole in the screen.*

BABY DOLL *calls anxiously, out of sight.*]

BABY DOLL: [*From kitchen*] *What's that?*

77]

THE PORCH.

[VACARRO *whistles loudly and casually on the porch. He now slips his fingers through the hole and lifts the latch.*]

78]

INTERIOR. KITCHEN OF MEIGHAN HOUSE. FULL SHOT.

[*Large, old-fashioned room with antiquated, but very capacious, equipment – large ice-box, large sinks and draining-boards, large stove converted to gas.*

BABY DOLL *stands in the middle of the floor with an apprehensive expression, but as* VACARRO *continues whistling on the porch, her usual placidity returns. She notices kettle of greens on the stove.*]

BABY DOLL: Stupid old thing – forgot to light the stove. [*She opens the ice-box for lemons.*] Git me a Frigidaire one of these days.

[*The pan under the ice-box has overflowed and is swamping the floor.*]

Got to empty that pan.

[*Pulls it from under refrigerator with a grunt. A sound catches her ear, a sharp, slapping sound. She looks up anxiously, but the sound is not repeated. She takes out lemons, leaves ice-box door hanging open. All her movements are fumbling and weak. She keeps rubbing her perspiring hands on her hips. She starts to cut lemon, the knife slips and cuts her finger. She looks at the finger. It looks all right at first, then a drop of blood appears. She whimpers a little. The blood increases. She begins to cry like a baby.*

She makes a vague, anxious movement. Again the slapping sound followed by a soft human sound like a chuckle. She looks that way. Cocks her head. But the sound is not repeated. Still squeezing the cut finger she begins to wander toward the front of the house.

CAMERA PANS WITH BABY DOLL AS SHE WANDERS THROUGH HOUSE.

She passes through a bare huge room with a dusty chandelier. It was the dining-room when the house belonged to the old plantation owners. She whimpers under her breath, squeezing the bleeding finger. Now the blood is running down the hand to the wrist and down the wrist to the forearm and trickling into the soft hollow of her elbow. She groans and whimpers at the sight of the great flight of stairs, but starts up them.

Half-way up, at the landing, she hears the slapping sound again and the faun-like mocking laughter. She stops there and waits and listens — but the sound isn't immediately repeated, so she goes on up. She goes into the bathroom and starts to bandage her cut finger.]

79]

INTERIOR HALL OF MEIGHAN HOUSE.
VACARRO DISCOVERED. FULL SHOT.

[VACARRO *is grinning up at the staircase. He slaps the banisters viciously with his whip, then chuckles.*

CAMERA PANS WITH VACARRO.

He strolls into the kitchen, sees ice-box door hanging open. Helps himself to the remains of a chicken, tearing it apart and gnawing the meat off it. He notices lemons and bloodspots – laughs.]

SILVA: Trail o' blood! Ha ha! [*He empties the flooded ice-pan over dirty dishes in sink.*] Filth! Disgusting! [*He slaps the wall with whip and laughs.*]

80]

INTERIOR. THE MEIGHANS' BEDROOM.
BABY DOLL WANDERS IN FROM BATHROOM.

[*The finger is clumsily bandaged now, and she wanders across the room and examines herself in the mirror.*]

BABY DOLL: Look a' me! Big mess. . . .

[*There are dark stains of sweat on the water-melon pink dress. She lazily starts to remove it. Hears the slapping sound and laugh closer. Pauses, her mouth hanging open. Fumbling attempt to lock door. Key slips from her weak, nerveless fingers. She stoops, grunting, to pick it up.*]

81]

INTERIOR KITCHEN.
VACARRO SQUEEZING LEMONS AND
HURLING THE RINDS SAVAGELY AWAY.

[*He finds gin bottle and sloshes gin into pitcher. Takes ice-pick and chops off big hunk of ice. He seems to enjoy all these physical activities, grins tightly, exposing his teeth. Sticks ice-pick into wall as if he were stabbing an enemy. Holds pitcher over his head whirling it rapidly so the drink sloshes over and ice rattles loudly, liquid running down his bare brown muscular arm. He drinks out of pitcher.*]

82]

INTERIOR BEDROOM. BABY DOLL IN DAMP
SLIP ROOTING IN CLOSET FOR A FRESH
DRESS.

[*She hears ice rattling in pitcher. Pauses. Cocks head, listening apprehensively. Makes sure door is locked.*]

83]

INTERIOR MEIGHANS' BEDROOM –
A DIFFERENT ANGLE. BABY DOLL.
[*Her slip hangs half off one great globular breast, gleaming with sweat. She listens intently.*]

84]

INTERIOR HALL AND STAIRWAY OF
MEIGHAN HOUSE. VACARRO SOFTLY
CLIMBING STAIRS.
*CAMERA FOLLOWS VACARRO INTO ROOMS
ACROSS HALL FROM BEDROOM – THEN
INTO CHILD'S NURSERY –*
[*Never used. Hobby horse, small fenced bed, Mother Goose pictures on wall. He sits astride wooden horse, lashes its rump with the whip and rocks on it.*]

85]

INTERIOR MEIGHANS' BEDROOM.
BABY DOLL SPRINGS UP FROM FLOOR.
[BABY DOLL *unlocks the door and peers anxiously into hall. The noise stops.*]
BABY DOLL: Archie Lee! Is that you?
[VACARRO (*out of sight*) *gives a soft wolf-whistle.*]
BABY DOLL: Who's that? Who's in there? [*She crosses the hall into nursery.*]

86]

INTERIOR NURSERY. VACARRO SLIPPING
INTO NEXT ROOM AS BABY DOLL ENTERS.
BABY DOLL: [*Nervously*] Hey! What's goin' on?
[*Whip slap and soft mocking laughter, barely audible.*]
BABY DOLL: Mr Vacarro? Are you in that room?
[*She crosses fearfully and enters next room,* VACARRO *slipping out just before her entrance. Now she is really frightened.*]

87]

INTERIOR EMPTY ROOM ADJOINING
NURSERY – FULL SHOT. BABY DOLL
ENTERS FEARFULLY.

BABY DOLL: You! Git outa my house! You got no right to
come in! Where are you?

   *[The door to the hall is locked. She hears the key turn in the lock.
Gasps. Pounds door. Rushes back panting into nursery.]*

88]

INTERIOR NURSERY. BABY DOLL RUSHES IN.

BABY DOLL: Mr Vacarro, stop playing hide-and-seek!

   [The soft mocking laughter comes from the hall.]

I know it's you! You're making me very nervous! Mr
Vacarro!! Mr Vacarro.... Mr Vacarro....

   *[With each call she creeps forward a few steps. All of a sudden
he springs at her, shouting –]*

SILVA: *[Sudden shout]* BOO!

   *[At this point the scene turns into a wild romp of children. She
shrieks with laughter. He howls, shouts. She shrieks with terror.
She giggles hysterically, running into the hall and starting down
steps. He leaps upon banister and slides to foot of stairs. She
turns on the stairs and runs through various rooms slamming
doors, giggling hysterically as she runs. A spirit of abandon
enters the flight and the pursuit. As he follows her into the
bedroom, she throws a pillow at him. He does a comic pratfall,
embracing the pillow. She shrieks with laughter. He lunges
toward her, throwing the pillow at her fugitive figure.
She is about to run downstairs, but he blocks the way. She
screams and takes the steps to the attic.]*

89]

INTERIOR ATTIC.

   *[Dusty late afternoon beams of light through tiny peaked
windows in gables and a jumble of discarded things that have the
poetry of things once lived with by the no-longer living.*

BABY DOLL *doesn't stop to observe all this. She probably didn't even expect to find herself in an attic. She rushes in, slams the door, discovers a rusty bolt and bolts it just as* VACARRO *arrives at the door.*

Her panting laughter expires as he pushes the door. She suddenly realizes the full import of her situation; gasps and backs away.]

SILVA: Open Sesame!!

BABY DOLL: [*In a low, serious voice*] The game is over. I've quit.

SILVA: That's not fair, you've got to keep playing hide-and-seek till you're it.

BABY DOLL: Mr Vacarro, will you please go back downstairs so I can unlock the door of this attic and come out – because the floor is weak. . . . I don't want to fall through. It's crumbling under my feet. I had no idea – I never been up here before! – it was in such a weaken condition. [*There is something appealing in her soft, pleasing voice.*]

SILVA: [*Whispering, mouth to crack*] I wouldn't dream of leaving you alone in a falling-down attic any more than you'd dream of eatin' a nut a man had cracked in his mouth. Don't you realize that??

BABY DOLL: [*With sudden gathering panic*] Mr Vacarro! I got to get out of here. Quick! Go! Go! – down! Quick, please!

SILVA: I can hear that old floor giving away fast. . . .

BABY DOLL: So can I, and I'm *on* it.

SILVA: Shall I call the fire department to come here with a net to catch you when you fall through?

BABY DOLL: Wouldn't be time. No! Go! – then I can unlock the –

SILVA: No, I don't suppose they'd get here on time or if they did the net would be rotten as those fire hoses last night when they came to put out the fire that burned down my gin!

[*Suddenly, a piece of plaster falls beneath her feet. The rotten laths are exposed. She scrambles to another place, which is – or seems – equally shaky. She screams.*]

SILVA: Are you being attacked by a ghost in there?

BABY DOLL: Please be kind! Go away!

SILVA: Why don't you unlock the door so I can come to your rescue?

BABY DOLL: I – can't because ...

SILVA: Huh? Huh?

BABY DOLL: [*Whisper*] YOU.

[VACARRO *shoves door just a little with his shoulder. The bolt is not strong.*]

You ... so! *Scare* me!

SILVA: Scared of *me*??

BABY DOLL: Yeah, scared of you and your – *whip*.

SILVA: Why're you scared of my whip? Huh? Do you think I might whip you? Huh? Scared I might whip you with it and

[*Slaps boots regularly with riding crop.*]

leave red marks on your – body, on your – creamy white silk – skin? Is that why're scared, Mrs Meighan?

[*A murmur from her.*]

You want me to go away – with my whip??

[*Another murmur.*]

All right. Tell you what I'm gonna do. I'm gonna slip pencil and paper under this door and all I want is your signature on the paper....

BABY DOLL: What paper?

SILVA: I guess that you would call it an affidavit, legally stating that Archie Lee Meighan burned down the Syndicate Gin.... [*Pause*] Okay?

BABY DOLL: Mr Vacarro, this whole floor's about to collapse under me!

SILVA: What do you say?

BABY DOLL: Just leave the paper, leave it right out there and I'll sign it and send it to you, I'll ...

SILVA: Mrs Meighan, I am a Sicilian. They're an old race of people, an ancient race, and ancient races aren't trustful races by nature. I've got to have the signed paper now. Otherwise I'm going to break this door down. Do you hear me? [*A pause*] Do you hear me?

[*Silence*]

[*Whimpering, sobbing.*] I gather you don't believe me.

[*Suddenly, with a single eloquent gesture of his whole body he has pushed the door open and on the other side* BABY DOLL, *in absolute panic, runs, runs away from the threatening man and whip and towards the darkest corner of the attic. A few steps, however, and the floor really gives way. There is a shower of plaster, a rising cloud of plaster dust.*

VACARRO's *face.*

The dust settles to reveal her, precariously perched across a beam . . .

VACARRO *calmly lights a cigarette.*]

SILVA: Now you're either going to agree to sign this thing, or I'm going to come out there after you and my additional weight will make the whole floor you know what!

BABY DOLL: OOOOOOH! What am I gonna do?

SILVA: Do what I tell you. [*He gingerly steps on a place. . . . A trickle of plaster*] Awful bad shape.

[*He reaches and picks up a 1 × 3 about twelve feet long. On the end of it he puts a pencil and piece of paper.*]

BABY DOLL: O-o-o-o-o-h!

SILVA: What? [*Suddenly, he stamps on the plaster. There is a big fall of plaster;* BABY DOLL *screams.*]

BABY DOLL: All right, all right. – All right. . . . Hurry! Hurry!

SILVA: Hurry what?

BABY DOLL: I'll do whatever you want – only hurry!!

SILVA: Here it comes. . . .

[*He reaches out his little piece of paper and pencil, balanced on the 1 × 3. She grabs it, scribbles her name in frantic haste, panting, and puts the piece of paper back, fixing it on a nail on the end of the 1 × 3, and* VACARRO *pulls it back. He looks at her signature and throws back his head in a sudden wild laugh.*]

SILVA: Thank you. You may come out now.

BABY DOLL: Not till I hear you! Going down those stairs. . . .

SILVA: [*Grinning and starting down*] Hear me? Hear my descending footsteps on the stairs. . . .

[VACARRO *straddles the long spiralled banister and slides all*

*the way down to the landing at the bottom with a leap that starts
another minor cascade.*

BABY DOLL *utters a little cry and comes out of the attic door.
Silence. Putt-putt-putt-putt of the gin. She leans over stair well
and looks straight down into the grinning face of* VACARRO.
He gives her a quick, grinning nod or salute.]

SILVA: Okay, you're 'Home free'! And so am I! Bye-bye!

BABY DOLL: Where are you going??

SILVA: Back to my little grey Quonset home in the West! For
a peaceful siesta. . . .

BABY DOLL: Wait, please! – I want to –

[*She starts to come running down the stairs, her hair wild,
panting, sweating, smeared with attic dust. Then half-way down
she stops. . . .*]

BABY DOLL: [*Now stealing towards him*] I want to –

[*But she can't remember what she 'wants to'. He waits quizzi-
cally with his cocky grin for her to complete her sentence but she
doesn't. Instead she looks up and down him and her eyelids
flutter as if the image could not be quietly contained.*

*He nods as if in agreement to something stated. He chuckles and
then turns on his heels and starts briskly for the porch. She calls
after him . . .*]

BABY DOLL: Was *that* all you wanted . . .?

[*He turns and looks at her.*]

Me to confess that Archie Lee burnt down your gin?

SILVA: What else did you imagine?

[*She turns away like a shy child, serious-faced; she sits down on
the bottom step.*]

SILVA: [*Gently*] You're a child, Mrs Meighan. That's why we
played hide-and-seek, a game for children. . . .

BABY DOLL: You don't have to go all the way to your place
for a nap. You could take a nap here.

SILVA: But all the furniture's been removed from the house.

BABY DOLL: Not the nursery stuff. They's a small bed in
there, a crib, you could curl up and – let the slats down. . . .

[*An effect of two shy children trying to strike up a friendship.
He continues to look at her. The windy afternoon has tossed a
cloud over the sun, now declining. But it passes and his smile*

68

becomes as warm as sunlight. She isn't looking into his face but down at the scuffed kid slippers. Abruptly he gives a short quick nod and says simply . . .

SILVA: I'm happy to accept the invitation. [*He starts up the stairs. When he gets to the point where she is sitting, he says*] Come up and sing me to sleep. [*Then he continues on up*]
[BABY DOLL *is left alone, bewildered, sitting alone on the big staircase.*]

BABY DOLL: [*To herself*] My daddy would *turn* in his *grave*. [*She starts up the stairs. . . .*]

90]

THE NURSERY.
[VACARRO *is on the crib, with the slats down. He is curled with his thumb in his mouth. She comes to view, stands in the doorway a moment, then goes and crouches beside the bed. Gently, she raises his head and bare throat, crooks an arm under and begins to sing,* 'Rock-a-Bye Baby'.
He sighs contentedly, removes the signed paper from his shirt pocket and tucks it under his belt for safer keeping.
Then he appears to fall asleep.]

DISSOLVE.

91]

IN A HOSPITAL ROOM.
[AUNT ROSE COMFORT *is sitting by a friend who is in her death coma.* AUNT ROSE *eating chocolate cherries.*]

DISSOLVE.

92]

SUPPLY STORE IN MEMPHIS. MEIGHAN AT COUNTER.
ARCHIE: [*To clerk*] Godamighty, man, I'm good for it.
[*He reaches for the part he has come for. It's wrapped and ready to go.*]

CLERK: We have orders. No credit. Cash basis. Everything.

ARCHIE: I warn you. I'll never come in this store again.

CLERK: Sorry.

ARCHIE: Look, I just happened to leave the place in my work clothes. My wallet ain't on me!

CLERK: Cash only.

[MR ARCHIE LEE MEIGHAN *suddenly turns and leaves in complete disgust.*]

93]

FRONT. ARCHIE LEE'S GIN.

[*It is several hours later and he has driven back from Memphis. He halts his motor with an exhausted grunt. He appears to have shrunk in size. He carries a sweat-drenched coat over his arm and the sweaty shirt clings to him. His chest heaves with unhealthy fast respiration, and he fingers the unbuttoned collar, as he takes in the situation. The gin is running again!!! – and without his O.K. – and how did they get the damned thing going again!!??*]

93A]

INTERIOR GIN.

[*He walks in and passes* ROCK.]

ARCHIE: Hahaha! Looks like we're back in business.

ROCK: [*Offers him only the most fleeting glance*] Does, doesn't it.

ARCHIE: You all must have done some mighty fast repairs.

ROCK: No repairs – put in a new saw-cylinder.

ARCHIE: From where? Out of a cloud? Why, I checked every supply outfit between Memphis and Greenville and nobody's got a new saw-cylinder ready for installation before next Wednesday.

ROCK: [*Tersely*] Boss had one at our place. I put it in.

ARCHIE: How do you like that? How come I wasn't let in on this piece of information before I lit out of here on the wild-goose chase that just about killed me? Where is that wop Vacarro? I want to get some explanation of this.

[*At this precise moment the whistle blows, announcing the end of the day and the gin machinery stops work. The Negroes, who have been working as porters and mechanics, line up for pay.*]

70

ROCK: [*Meantime*] You seen the boss-man, Norm?
  [*A Negro shakes his head.*
  ROCK *notices* ARCHIE *looking at the line a little worried.*]
ROCK: [*To* ARCHIE] Don't worry. Vacarro is meeting the pay-roll for tonight.
ARCHIE: Where is he?
ROCK: [*To another Negro*] Moose, you seen the boss?
MOOSE: No time lately, Capt'n.

94]

THE GIN. (ANOTHER ANGLE)
  [MEIGHAN *retreats from the gin uncertainly. Camera follows. Half-way across the road he hears laughter, evidently directed at him. His back stiffens. Something has happened, he feels, that has somehow made him the patsy of whatever occasion this is.*]

95]

CLOSE SHOT. MEIGHAN.
  [*Suspicious, angry, something violent and dangerous is growing up in his heart. He mutters to himself. Hears the laughter again. Curses to himself.*]

96]

MEIGHAN ENTERS THE BIG FRONT YARD
AND STARES AT THE HOUSE.

97]

THE HOUSE.
  [*Silent. Not a move. Not a sound.*]

98]

MEIGHAN NOTICES VACARRO'S
DISCARDED SHIRT.
  [*He picks it up and lifts his head and calls into the house.*]

ARCHIE: Hey! Anybody living here? Anybody still living in this house?

99]

UPSTAIRS. THE NURSERY.

[BABY DOLL, *considerably disarrayed, has heard* ARCHIE's *shout from below and is just making her way on hands and knees to the window. Now she crawls on the floor over to the crib.*]

BABY DOLL: It's Archie Lee.

[*Downstairs screen door slams.* VACARRO *gurgles, murmurs, whimpers, all of which mean 'don't bother me, I want to sleep'. There is a sudden shout from downstairs as if a cry of pain.*]

100]

DOWNSTAIRS.

[*What* MEIGHAN *sees is the debris of the ceiling. He looks up at the gaping hole in the roof over his head at the top of the stair well and then down the stairs.* BABY DOLL *appears on the staircase in a silken wrapper.*]

ARCHIE: *What happened here?*

[BABY DOLL *doesn't answer. She stares at him with blank insolence.*]

ARCHIE: Hunh? I said what the hell happened here?

BABY DOLL: You mean that mess in the hall? The plaster broke in the attic.

ARCHIE: How'd that – how'd that – happen?

BABY DOLL: How does anything happen? It just happened.

[*She comes on lazily down, avoiding his look.*]

101]

INTERIOR NIGHT. DOWNSTAIRS. FRONT HALL.

ARCHIE: Ain't I told you not to slop around here in a slip?

[*She gives a faint indifferent shrug which enrages him; he senses something openly contemptuous, a change in her attitude towards him. He grabs her bare shoulder.*]

What's the matter with your skin? It looks all broke out. [*Inspects the inflamed welts*]

What's this?

BABY DOLL: What's what?

ARCHIE: These marks on you?

BABY DOLL: Mosquito bites, I scratched them. . . . Lemme go.

ARCHIE: [*Bellowing*] Ain't I told you not to slop around here in a slip???!!!

[AUNT ROSE COMFORT, *alarmed by the shout, appears in door to kitchen, crying out thin and high.*]

AUNT ROSE: Almost ready, now, folks, almost ready!!

[*She rushes back into the kitchen with her frightened cackle. There is a crash of china from the kitchen.*]

ARCHIE: The breakage alone in that kitchen would ruin a well-to-do-man! Now you go up and git some decent clo'se on yuh an' come back down. Y'know they got a new bureau in Washington, D.C. It's called the U.W. Bureau. Y'know what U.W. stands for? It stands fo' useless women. They's secret plans on foot to round 'em all up and shoot 'em. Hahahaha!

BABY DOLL: How about men that's destructive? Don't they have secret plans to round up men that's destructive and shoot them too?

ARCHIE: What destructive men you talkin' about?

BABY DOLL: Men that blow things up and burn things down because they're too evil and stupid to git along otherwise. Because fair competition is too much for 'em. So they turn criminal. Do things like Arson. Wilful destruction of property by fire. . . . [*She steps out on the porch. Night sounds. A cool breeze tosses her damp curls. She sniffs the night air like a young horse. . . . The porch light, a milky globe patterned with dead insects, turns on directly over her head and* ARCHIE LEE *comes up behind her and grips her bare shoulders, his face anxious, cunning.*]

ARCHIE: Who said that to you? Where'd you git that from??

BABY DOLL: Turn that porch light off. There's men on the road can see me.

ARCHIE: Who said *arson* to you? Who spoke of wilful destruction of ... YOU never knew them words. Who SAID 'em to yuh?

BABY DOLL: Sometimes, Big Shot, you don't seem t' give me credit for much intelligence! I've been to school, in my life, and I'm a – magazine reader!

[*She shakes off his grip and starts down porch steps. There is a group of men on Tiger Tail Road. One of them gives a wolf-whistle. At once,* ARCHIE LEE *charges down the steps and across the yard towards the road – crying out –*

ARCHIE: *Who gave that whistle??* Which of you give a wolf-whistle at my wife?

[*The group ignores him except for a light mocking laugh as they continue down road. The Camera returns to* BABY DOLL *blandly smiling.*

We hear the rattle of the cistern pump being vigorously exercised in the side yard. ARCHIE LEE *stalks back up to porch, winded, like an old hound.* . . .]

ARCHIE: Men from the Syndicate *Plantation! White an' black* mixed! Headed fo' Tiger Tail Bayou with frog gigs and rubber boots on! I just hope they turn downstream and trespass across my property! I just hope they dast to! I'll blast them out of the Bayou with a shotgun!

BABY DOLL: Small dogs have a loud bark.

ARCHIE: Nobody's gonna insult no woman of *mine*!!

BABY DOLL: You take a lot for granted when you say *mine*. This afternoon I come to you for protection. What did I *git*? *Slapped!* And told to go home. . . . I, for one, have got no sympathy for you, now or ever. An' the rasslin' match between us is *over* so let me *go*!

ARCHIE: You're darn tootin' it's over. In just three hours the terms of the agreement will be settled for good.

BABY DOLL: Don't count on it. That agreement is cancelled. Because it takes two sides to make an agreement, like an argument, and both sides got to live up to it completely. You didn't live up to yours. Stuck me in a house which is haunted and five complete sets of unpaid-for furniture was removed from it las' night, OOHH I'm *free* from my side of that bargain!

ARCHIE: *Sharp at midnight!* We'll find out about that.

BABY DOLL: Too much has happened here lately. . . .

[*She descends into yard.* ARCHIE LEE *eyes her figure, sweating, licking his chops.*]

ARCHIE: Well . . . my credit's wide open again!

BABY DOLL: So is the jail-house door wide open for you if the truth comes out.

ARCHIE: You threatenin' me with – *blackmail*??

BABY DOLL: Somebody's drawin' some cool well water from the pump back there.

[*She starts back. He follows. The full frog-gigging moon emerges from a mackerel sky, and we see* VACARRO *making his ablutions at the cistern pump with the zest and vigour of a man satisfied.*]

BABY DOLL: [*With unaccustomed hilarity*] HEIGH-HO SILVER . . . HaHa!!

[ARCHIE LEE *stops dead in his tracks.*]

ARCHIE: Him?! Still on the place?

BABY DOLL: Give me another drink of that sweet well water, will yuh, Mistuh Vacarro? You're the first person could draw it.

ARCHIE: [*Advancing*] YOU STILL HERE?

BABY DOLL: Archie Lee, Mr Vacarro says he might not put up a new cotton gin, but let you gin cotton for him all the time, now. Ain't you pleased about that? Tomorrow he plans to come with lots more cotton, maybe another twenty-seven wagon-loads. And while you're ginning it out, he'll have me entertain him, make lemonade for him. It's going to go on and on! Maybe even next fall.

SILVA: [*Through the water*] Good neighbour policy in practice. [*Having wetted himself down he now drinks from gourd*] I love well water. It tastes as fresh as if it never was tasted before. Mrs Meighan, would you care for some, too?

BABY DOLL: Why thank you, yes, I would. [*There is a grace and sweetness and softness of speech about her, unknown before. . . .*]

75

SILVA: Cooler nights have begun.

[ARCHIE LEE *has been regarding the situation, with its various possibilities, and is far from content.*]

ARCHIE: How long you been on the place?

SILVA: [*Drawling sensuously with eyes on girl*] All this unusually long hot fall afternoon I've imposed on your hospitality. You want some of this well water?

ARCHIE: [*With a violent gesture of refusal*] Where you been here???

SILVA: Taking a nap on your only remaining bed. The crib in the nursery with the slats let down. I had to curl up on it like a pretzel, but the fire last night deprived me of so much sleep that almost any flat surface was suitable for slumber.

[*Winks impertinently at* ARCHIE LEE, *then turns to grin sweetly at* BABY DOLL, *wiping the drippings of well water from his throat. Then turns back to* ARCHIE]

But there's something sad about it. Know what I mean?

ARCHIE: Sad about what??

SILVA: An unoccupied nursery in a house, and all the other rooms empty. . . .

ARCHIE: That's no problem of yours!

SILVA: The good-neighbour policy makes your problems mine – and vice versa. . . .

AUNT ROSE: [*Violent and high and shrill, from the back steps*] SUPPER! READY! CHILDREN. . . . [*She staggers back in.*]

[*Now there's a pause in which all three stand tense and silent about the water pump.* BABY DOLL *with her slow, new smile speaks up first. . . .*]

BABY DOLL: You all didn't hear us called in to supper?

ARCHIE: You gonna eat here tonight?

SILVA: Mrs Meighan asked me to stay for supper but I told her I'd better get to hear the invitation from the head of the house before I'd feel free to accept it. So . . . What do you say?

[*A tense pause . . . then, with great difficulty . . .*]

ARCHIE: Stay! . . . fo' supper.

BABY DOLL: You'll have to take pot luck.

SILVA: I wouldn't be putting you out?

76

[*This is addressed to* BABY DOLL, *who smiles vaguely and starts toward the house, saying . . .*]

BABY DOLL: I better get into mu' clo'se. . . .

ARCHIE: Yeah . . . hunh. . . .

[*They follow her sensuous departure with their eyes till she fades into the dusk.*]

ARCHIE: Did I understand you to say you wouldn't build a new gin but would leave your business to me?

SILVA: If that's agreeable with you. . . .

ARCHIE: [*Turning from his wife's back to* VACARRO's *face*] I don't know yet, I'll have to consider the matter. . . . Financing is involved such as – new equipment. . . . Let's go in and eat now. I got a pain in my belly, I got a sort of heartburn. . . .

102]

INTERIOR HOUSE.

[*They enter the kitchen and then to the dining-room.* ARCHIE LEE's *condition is almost shock. He can't quite get with the situation. He numbly figures that he'd better play it cool till the inner fog clears. But his instinct is murder. His cowardly caution focuses his malice on the old woman and the unsatisfactory supper she's prepared.*]

ARCHIE: Hey! Hey! One more place at the table! Mr Vacarro from the Syndicate Plantation is stayin' to supper.

AUNT ROSE: [*With a startled outcry, clutching her chest*] Oh – I had no idea that company was expected. Just let me – change the silver and . . .

ARCHIE: Another place is all that's called for. Have you been here all day?

AUNT ROSE: What was that, Archie Lee?

ARCHIE: HAVE YOU BEEN IN THE HOUSE ALL AFTERNOON OR DID YOU LIGHT OUT TO THE COUNTY HOSPITAL TO EAT SOME CHOCOLATE CANDY????

[AUNT ROSE *gasps as if struck, then she cackles . . .*]

AUNT ROSE: I – I – visited! – an old friend in a – coma!

ARCHIE: Then you was out while I was – . [*Turns to* VACARRO – *fiercely*] I work like the hammers of hell! I come home to find the attic floor fell through, my wife bad-tempered, insulting! and a supper of hog slops – . Sit down, eat. I got to make a phone call.

[*He crosses somewhat unsteadily into the hall and picks up the telephone as* BABY DOLL *descends the grand staircase and goes past him with her face austerely averted. She is clad in a fresh silk sheath and is adjusting an earring as she passes through the hall. We go with her into dining-room.*]

BABY DOLL: He's at the phone about something and if I was you, I wouldn't hang around long.

SILVA: I think I've got the ace of spades in my pocket. [*He pats where he's stashed the confession signed by* BABY DOLL.]

BABY DOLL: Don't count on a law court. Justice is deaf and blind as that old woman!

[AUNT ROSE COMFORT *rushes out to cut roses for a vase to set on table.*]

BABY DOLL: I'm advising you, go! – while he's on the phone.

SILVA: I find you different this evening in some way.

BABY DOLL: Never mind, just go! Before he gits off the phone.

SILVA: Suddenly grown up!

BABY DOLL: [*Looking at him gratefully*] I feel cool and rested, for the first time in my life. I feel that way, rested and cool. [*A pause*] Are you going or staying???

[*They are close together by table. Suddenly she catches her breath and flattens her body to his. The embrace is active. She reaches above her and pulls the beaded chain of the light bulb, plunging the room in dark. We hear two things, the breath of the embracing couple and the voice of* ARCHIE LEE *on the phone.*]

ARCHIE: A bunch of men from the Syndicate Plantation are out frog-giggin' on Tiger Tail Bayou and I thought we all might join the party. How's about meeting at the Brite Spot in halfn hour? With full equipment.

[*A few more indistinct words, he hangs up. The light is switched back on in the dining-room.* AUNT ROSE *rushes in.*]

AUNT ROSE: Roses! Poems of nature . . .

78

[ARCHIE LEE *enters from the hall. His agitation is steadily mounting.*]

ARCHIE: Never mind poems of nature, just put food on th' table!

AUNT ROSE: If I'd only known that company was expected, I'd ... [*Her breathless voice expires as she scuttles about putting roses in a vase.*]

AUNT ROSE: Only take a minute.

ARCHIE: We ain't waitin' no minute. Bring out the food. ...
    [BABY DOLL *smiles, rather scornfully, at* ARCHIE LEE *bullying the old woman.*]

ARCHIE: Is that what they call a Mona Lisa smile you got on your puss?

BABY DOLL: Don't pick on Aunt Rose. ...

ARCHIE: [*Shouting*] Put some food on the table!! [*Then muttering dangerously*] I'm going to have a talk with that old woman, right here tonight. She's outstayed her welcome.

SILVA: What a pretty blue wrapper you're wearing tonight, Mrs Meighan.

BABY DOLL: [*Coyly*] Thank you, Mr Vacarro.

SILVA: There's so many shades of blue. Which shade is that?

BABY DOLL: Just baby blue.

ARCHIE: Baby blue, huh!

SILVA: It brings out the blue of your eyes.

ARCHIE: [*Screaming*] Food! Food!

AUNT ROSE: Immediately! This instant!
    [*She comes through door from the kitchen, holding a big plate of greens, which she sets on the table with great apprehension. They are not really cooked.* ARCHIE *stares at them.*]

103]

CLOSE SHOT OF GREENS, WHICH ARE ALMOST RAW.

104]

CLOSE SHOT OF ARCHIE SWEARING UNDER HIS BREATH.

GROUP SCENE.

BABY DOLL: This wrapper was part of my trousseau, as a matter of fact. I got all my trousseau at Memphis at various departments where my daddy was known. Big department stores on Main Street.

ARCHIE: WHAT IS THIS STUFF??!! GRASS??!!

BABY DOLL: Greens! Don't you know greens when you see them?

ARCHIE: This stuff is greens??!!

[AUNT ROSE *comes nervously from pantry.*]

AUNT ROSE: Archie Lee dotes on greens, don't you, Archie Lee?

ARCHIE: No, I don't.

AUNT ROSE: You don't? You don't dote on greens?

ARCHIE: I don't think I ever declared any terrible fondness for greens in your presence.

AUNT ROSE: Well, somebody did.

ARCHIE: Somebody probably did – sometime, somewhere, but that don't mean it was me!

[*Lurches back in his chair and half rises, swinging to face* VACARRO–*who had taken* BABY DOLL'*s hand under the table.* VACARRO *smiles blandly.*]

BABY DOLL: Sit back down, Big Shot, an' eat your greens. Greens put iron in the system.

AUNT ROSE: I thought that Archie Lee doted on greens! – All those likes an' dislikes are hard to keep straight in your head. But Archie Lee's easy to cook for. Jim's a complainer, oh, my, what a complainer Jim is, and Susie's household, they're nothing but complainers.

ARCHIE: *Take this slop off th' table!!*

AUNT ROSE: [*Terrified*] I'll – cook you some – eggs Birmingham! – These greens didn' cook long enough. I played a fool trick with my stove. I forgot to light it! Ha ha! When I went out to the store – I had my greens on the stove. I thought I'd left 'em boilin'. But when I got home I discovered that my stove wasn't lighted.

ARCHIE: Why do you say 'my' stove? Why is everything 'my'?

BABY DOLL: Archie Lee, I believe you been drinkin'!

ARCHIE: You keep out of this! Set down, Aunt Rose.

AUNT ROSE: – Do what, Archie Lee?

ARCHIE: Set down here. I want to ask you a question. [AUNT ROSE *sits down slowly and stiffly, all a-tremble.*] What sort of – plans have you made?

AUNT ROSE: Plans, Archie Lee? What sort of plans do you mean?

ARCHIE: Plans for the future!

BABY DOLL: I don't think this kind of discussion is necessary in front of company.

SILVA: Mr Meighan, when a man is feeling uncomfortable over something, it often happens that he takes out his annoyance on some completely innocent person just because he has to make somebody suffer.

ARCHIE: You keep outa this, too. I'm askin' Aunt Rose a perfectly sensible question. Now, Aunt Rose. You been here since August and that's a mighty long stay. Now, it's my honest opinion that you're in need of a rest. You been cookin' around here and cooking' around there for how long now? How long have you been cookin' around people's houses?

AUNT ROSE: [*Barely able to speak*] I've helped out my – relatives, my – folks – whenever they – *needed me to*! I was always – *invited*! Sometimes – *begged* to come! When *babies* were expected or when somebody was *sick*, they called for Aunt Rose, and Aunt Rose was always – ready.... Nobody *ever* had to – *put me – out*! If you – gentlemen will excuse me from the table – I will pack my things! If I hurry I'll catch the nine o'clock bus to – [*She can't think 'where to'.* VACARRO *seizes her hand, pushing back from table.*]

SILVA: Miss Rose Comfort. Wait. I'll drive you home.

AUNT ROSE: – I don't! – have nowhere to! – go....

SILVA: Yes, you do. I need someone to cook for me at my place. I'm tired of my own cooking and I am anxious to try those eggs Birmingham you mentioned. Is it a deal?

AUNT ROSE: – Why, I –

BABY DOLL: Sure it's a deal. Mr Vacarro will be good to you, Aunt Rose Comfort, and he will even *pay* you, and maybe – well – y'never can tell about things in the future. . . .

AUNT ROSE: *I'll run pack my things!*
[*She resumes reedy hymn in a breathless, cracked voice as she goes upstairs.*]

ARCHIE: Anything else around here you wanta take with yuh, Vacarro?

SILVA:
[*Looks around coolly as if considering the question*]

BABY DOLL:
[*Utters a high, childish giggle*]

ARCHIE: Well, *is* they? Anything else around here you wanta take away with yuh?

BABY DOLL: [*Rising gaily*] Why, yaiss, Archie Lee. Mr Vacarro noticed the house was overloaded with furniture and he would like us to loan him five complete sets of it to –

ARCHIE: [*Seizing neck of whiskey bottle*] YOU SHUDDUP! I will git to you later.

BABY DOLL: If you ever git to me it sure is going to be *later*, ha, ha, *much* later, ha ha!
[*She crosses to kitchen sink, arranging her kiss-me-quicks in the soap-splashed mirror, also regarding the two men behind her with bland satisfaction; her childish face, beaming, is distorted by the flared glass.*
She sings or hums 'Sweet and Lovely'. ARCHIE LEE *stands by table, breathing heavy as a walrus in labour. He looks from one to the other.* SILVA *coolly picks up a big kitchen knife and lops off a hunk of bread, then tosses kitchen knife out of* ARCHIE LEE's *reach and then he dips bread in pot of greens.*]

SILVA: Coloured folks call this pot liquor.

BABY DOLL: I love pot liquor.

SILVA: Me, too.

BABY DOLL: [*Dreamily*] – Crazy 'bout pot liquor. . . .
[*She turns about and rests her hips against sink.* ARCHIE

LEE's *breathing is loud as a cotton gin, his face fiery. He takes swallow after swallow from bottle.*

VACARRO *devours bread.*]

SILVA: Mm-ummm!

BABY DOLL: Good?

SILVA: *Yes! – Good!*

BABY DOLL: – *That's* good. . . .

[OLD FUSSY *makes a slow stately entrance, pushing the door open wider with her fat hips and squawking peevishly at this slight inconvenience.*

MEIGHAN *wheels about violently and hurls empty bottle at her. She flaps and squawks back out. Her distressed outcries are taken up by her sisters, who are sensibly roosting.*]

BABY DOLL: [*Giggling*] Law! Ole Fussy mighty near made it that time! Why, that old hen was comin' in like she'd been invited t'supper.

[*Her giggly voice expires as* MEIGHAN *wheels back around and bellows.*

ARCHIE LEE *explodes volcanically. His violence should give him almost a Dostoevskian stature.*

It builds steadily through scene as a virtual lunacy possesses him with realization of his hopeless position.]

ARCHIE: OH HO HO HO HO HO! [*Kicks kitchen door shut*] Now you all listen to me! Quit giving looks back an' forth an' listen to me! Y'think I'm deaf, dumb an' blind, or somethin', do yuh? You're *mistook.* Oh, brother, but you're much, much – *mistook!* Ohhhh, I knooow! – I guess I look like a – I guess I look like a – [*Panting, puffing pause; he reels a little, clutching chair back.*]

BABY DOLL: [*Insolently childish lisp*] What d'you guess you look like, Archie Lee? Y'was about t' tell us an' then yuh quit fo' some –

ARCHIE: *Yeah, yeah, yeah!* Some little innocent Baby Doll of a wife not ready fo' marriage, oh, no, not yet ready for marriage but plenty ready t'– Oh, I see how it's funny, I can see how it's funny, I see the funny side of it. *Oh ho ho ho ho!* Yes, it sure is comic, comic as hell! But there's one little *teensy-eensy* little – thing that you – *overlooked!* I! Got

position! Yeah, yeah, *I* got *position*! Here in this county!
Where I was bo'n an' brought up! I hold a respected
position, lifelong! – member of – Wait! Wait! – Baby
Doll. . . .

[*She had started to cross past him; he seizes her wrist. She
wrenches free.* VACARRO *stirs and tenses slightly but doesn't
rise or change his cool smile.*]

On my side 're friends, long-standin' *bus'ness* associates, an'
social! See what I mean? You ain't got that advantage, have
you, mister? Huh, mister? Ain't you a dago, or something,
excuse me, I mean Eyetalian or something, here in Tiger
Tail County?

SILVA: Meighan, I'm not a doctor, but I was a medical corps-
man in the Navy and you've got a very unhealthy looking
flush on your face right now which is almost purple as a –
[*He was going to say 'baboon's behind'.*]

ARCHIE: [*Bellowing out*] ALL I GOT TO DO IS GIT ON THAT
PHONE IN THE HALL!

SILVA: And call an ambulance from the county hospital?

ARCHIE: Hell, I don't even need t' make a phone call! I can
handle this situation *m'self*! – with legal protection that no
one could –

SILVA: [*Still coolly*] What situation do you mean, Meighan?

ARCHIE: Situation which I come home to find here under my
roof! Oh, I'm not such a marble-missing old fool! – I
couldn't size it up! – I sized it up the moment I seen you
was still on this place and *her*! – with that *sly smile on her*!
[*Takes a great swallow of liquor from the fresh bottle*] And *you*
with *yours* on *you*! I know how to wipe off both of those
sly – !

[*Crosses to closet door.* BABY DOLL *utters a gasp and signals*
VACARRO *to watch out.*]

SILVA: Meighan? [*He speaks coolly, almost with a note of sympathy*] *You* know, and *I* know, and I *know* that you *know*
that I *know*! – That you set fire to my cotton gin last night.
You burnt down the Syndicate Gin and I got in my pocket
a signed affidavit, a paper, signed by a witness, whose
testimony will even hold up in the law courts of Tiger Tail

County! – That's all I come here for and that's all I got ...
whatever else you suspect – well! you're mistaken. ... Isn't
that so, Mrs Meighan? Isn't your husband mistaken in
thinking that I got anything out of this place but this
signed affidavit which was the purpose of my all-afternoon
call?

[*She looks at him, angry, hurt.*

MEIGHAN *wheels about, panting.*]

SILVA: [*Continuing*] Yes, I'm foreign but I'm not revengeful,
Meighan, at least not more than is rightful. [*Smiles sweetly*]
– I think we got a workable good-neighbour policy between
us. It might work out, anyhow I think it deserves a try.
Now as to the other side of the situation, which I don't have
to mention. Well, all I can say is, a certain attraction –
exists! Mutually, I believe! But nothing's been rushed. I
needed a little shut-eye after last night's – excitement. I
took a nap upstairs in the nursery crib with the slats let
down to accommodate my fairly small frame, and I have
faint recollection of being sung to by someone – a lullaby
song that was – sweet ... [*His voice is low, caressing*] – and the
touch of – cool fingers, but that's all, absolutely!

ARCHIE: Y'think I'm gonna put up with this – ?

SILVA: Situation? You went to a whole lot of risk an'
trouble to get my business back. Now don't you want it?
It's up to you, Archie Lee, it's –

ARCHIE: COOL! Yeah, cool, very cool!

SILVA: – The heat of the fire's died down. ...

ARCHIE: UH – HUH! YOU'VE FIXED YOUR WAGON WITH
THIS SMART TALK, YOU JUST NOW FIXED YOUR
WAGON! I'M GONNA MAKE A PHONE CALL THAT'LL
WIPE THE GRIN OFF YOUR GREASY WOP FACE FOR
GOOD! [*He charges into hall and seizes phone.*]

SILVA: [*Crossing to* BABY DOLL *at kitchen sink*] Is my wop face
greasy, Mrs Meighan?

[*She remains at mirror but her childish smile fades; her face goes
vacant and blind; she suddenly tilts her head back against the bare
throat of the man standing behind her. Her eyes clenched shut. ...
His eyelids flutter as his body presses against all the mindless*

85

virgin softness of her abundant young flesh. We can't see their
hands, but hers are stretched behind her, his before him.]

106]

HALL.

ARCHIE: [*Bellowing like a steer*] I WANT SPOT, MIZZ HOPKINS,
WHE' IS SPOT!?

107]

BABY DOLL WITH VACARRO.

BABY DOLL: I think you better go 'way. . . .

SILVA: I'm just waiting to take you girls away with me. . . .

BABY DOLL: [*Softly as in a dream*] Yeah. I'm goin' too. I'll
check in at the Kotton King Hotel and – Now I better go
up an' – he'p Aunt Rose Comfo't pack. . . .

[*Releases herself regretfully from the embrace and crosses into
hall.*]

108]

HALL. CLOSE SHOT OF SILVA LOOKING
AFTER HER. IN THE HALL SHE UTTERS A
SHARP OUTCRY AS MEIGHAN STRIKES AT
HER.

BABY DOLL: YOU GONNA BE SORRY FOR EV'RY TIME YOU
LAID YOUR UGLY OLE HANDS ON ME, YOU STINKER,
YOU! YOU STINKING STINKER, STINKERRR!

[*Her footsteps running upstairs.* VACARRO *chuckles almost
silently and goes quietly out the back door.*]

109]

THE YARD.

[VACARRO *crosses through a yard littered with uncollected
garbage, tin cans, refuse.* . . .]

110]

HALL. MEIGHAN REMOVES SHOTGUN FROM
CLOSET.

111]

YARD. CUT BACK TO EXTERIOR.

[*Crooked moon beams fitfully through a racing mackerel sky, the air full of motion.*

VACARRO *picks his way fastidiously among the refuse, wades through the tall seeding grass, into the front yard. Clutches the lower branch of a pecan tree and swings up into it. Cracks a nut between his teeth as –*]

ARCHIE: [*Shouting and blundering through the house*] HEY! WHERE YOU HIDING? WHERE YOU HIDING, WOP?!

112]

HOUSE. CLOSE SHOT OF MEIGHAN WITH SHOTGUN AND LIQUOR BOTTLE, ALREADY STUMBLING DRUNK....

113]

YARD. EXTERIOR NIGHT. VACARRO IN TREE. VOICE OF BABY DOLL AT PHONE.

BABY DOLL: I want the Police Chief. Yes, the Chief, not just the police, the Chief. This is Baby Doll McCorkle speaking, the ex-Mrs Meighan on Tiger Tail Road! My husband has got a shotgun and is threat'nin' to –

[*Her voice turns into a scream. She comes running out front door followed by* MEIGHAN. *She darts around side of house.* MEIGHAN *is very drunk now. He goes the opposite way around the house.* VACARRO *drops out of tree and gives* BABY DOLL *a low whistle. She rushes back to front yard.*]

BABY DOLL: *Oh, Gah, Gah, watch out, he's got a shotgun. He's – crazy! I callt th' Chief of –*

[VACARRO *leaps into tree again.*]

SILVA: Grab my hand! Quick! Now *up! Up,* now Baby Doll!

[*He hoists her into tree with him as the wild-eyed old bull comes charging back around house with his weapon. He blasts away at a shadow. (Yard is full of windy shadows.) He is sobbing.*]

ARCHIE: BABY DOLL! BABY! BABY! BABY DOLL! MY BABY.

[*Goes stumbling around back of house, great wind in the trees.*
BABY DOLL *rests in the arms of* VACARRO.
MEIGHAN *in back yard. Storm cellar door bangs open.*
MEIGHAN *fires through it. Then at chicken coop. Then into
wheelless limousine chassis in side yard, etc., etc.*
Shot of VACARRO *and* BABY DOLL *in fork of pecan tree.*]

SILVA: [*Grinning*] We're still playing hide-and-seek!

BABY DOLL: [*Excitedly, almost giggling*] How long you guess
we gonna be up this tree?

SILVA: I don't care. I'm *comfortable* – Are you?

[*Her answer is a sigh. He cracks a nut in his mouth and divides it
with her. She giggles and whispers, 'Shhhh!'*]

ARCHIE: [*Raving, sobbing, stumbling*] Baby, my baby, oh, Baby
Doll, my baby.... *Silence.* HEY! WOP! YELLOWBELLY!
WHERE ARE YUH?

[AUNT ROSE COMFORT *comes forlornly out on the porch,
weighed down by ancient suitcase, roped together.*]

AUNT ROSE: [*Fearfully, her hair blown wild by the wind*] Baby
Doll, honey? Honey? Baby Doll, honey?

ARCHIE: [*In back yard*] I SEE YOU! COME OUT OF THERE,
YOU YELLOWBELLY WOP, YOU!

[*Shotgun blasts away behind house.* AUNT ROSE COMFORT
*on front porch utters a low cry and drops her suitcase. Backs
against wall, hand to chest.*
Fade in police siren approaching down Tiger Tail Road.]

BABY DOLL: [*Nestling in* VACARRO's *arms in tree*] I feel sorry
for poor old Aunt Rose Comfort. She doesn't know where
to go or what to do....

[*Moon comes briefly out and shines on their crouched figures in
fork on tree.*]

SILVA: [*Gently*] Does anyone know where to go, or what to
do?

114]

THE YARD. ANOTHER ANGLE. POLICE CAR
STOPPING BEFORE THE HOUSE AND MEN
JUMPING OUT.

[*Shot of* MEIGHAN *staggering and sobbing among the litter of uncollected garbage.*]

ARCHIE: Baby Doll, my baby! Yellow son of a –

115]

THE YARD. ANOTHER ANGLE. SHOT OF
AUNT ROSE COMFORT RETREATING INTO
SHADOW AS POLICE COME AROUND THE
HOUSE SUPPORTING ARCHIE LEE'S LIMP
FIGURE. SHOT OF COUPLE IN TREE AS
MOON GOES BACK OF CLOUDS.

[*Stillness. Dark.* AUNT ROSE COMFORT *begins to sing a hymn*: '*Rock of Ages*'.]

AUNT ROSE: Rock of ages, cleft for me,
          Let me hide myself in Thee!

[VACARRO *drops out of tree and stands with arms lifted for* BABY DOLL.]

SOMETHING UNSPOKEN

AND

SUDDENLY LAST SUMMER

Suddenly Last Summer and *Something Unspoken* were presented together under the collective title of *Garden District* at the York Theatre on First Avenue in New York on 7 January 1958, by John C. Wilson and Warner Le Roy. It was directed by Herbert Machiz; the stage set was designed by Robert Soule and the costumes by Stanley Simmons. Lighting was by Lee Watson and the incidental music by Ned Rorem. The cast was as follows:

Something Unspoken

CORNELIA SCOTT	Eleanor Phelps
GRACE LANCASTER	Hortense Alden

Suddenly Last Summer

MRS VENABLE	Hortense Alden
DR CUKROWICZ	Robert Lansing
MISS FOXHILL	Donna Cameron
MRS HOLLY	Eleanor Phelps
GEORGE HOLLY	Alan Mixon
CATHARINE HOLLY	Anne Meacham
SISTER FELICITY	Nanon-Kiam

The first British production of *Garden District* was presented at the Arts Theatre, London on 16 September 1958, under the direction of Herbert Machiz. The cast was as follows:

Something Unspoken

CORNELIA SCOTT	Beryl Measor
GRACE LANCASTER	Beatrix Lehmann

Suddenly Last Summer

MRS VENABLE	Beatrix Lehmann
DR CUKROWICZ	David Cameron
MISS FOXHILL	Margo Johns
MRS HOLLY	Beryl Measor
GEORGE HOLLY	Philip Bond
CATHARINE HOLLY	Patricia Neal
SISTER FELICITY	Gwen Nelson

To
Anne Meacham

SOMETHING UNSPOKEN

[MISS CORNELIA SCOTT, 60, *a wealthy Southern spinster,
is seated at a small mahogany table which is set for two. The
other place, not yet occupied, has a single rose in a crystal vase
before it.* MISS SCOTT's *position at the table is flanked by a
cradle phone, a silver tray of mail, and an ornate silver coffee urn.
An imperial touch is given by purple velvet drapes directly
behind her figure at the table. A console phonograph is at edge of
lighted area.*
At rise she is dialling a number on the phone.]

CORNELIA: Is this Mrs Horton Reid's residence? I am calling
for Miss Cornelia Scott. Miss Scott is sorry that she will not
be able to attend the meeting of the Confederate Daughters
this afternoon as she woke up this morning with a sore
throat and has to remain in bed, and will you kindly give
her apologies to Mrs Reid for not letting her know sooner.
Thank you. Oh, wait a moment! I think Miss Scott has
another message.
 [GRACE LANCASTER *enters the lighted area.* CORNELIA
 raises her hand in a warning gesture.]
– What is it, Miss Scott?
 [*Brief pause.*]
Oh. Miss Scott would like to leave word for Miss Esmeralda Hawkins to call her as soon as she arrives. Thank you.
Goodbye. [*Hangs up.*] You see I am having to impersonate
my secretary this morning!
GRACE: The light was so dim it didn't wake me up.
 [*Grace Lancaster is 40 or 45, faded, but still pretty. Her blonde
 hair, greying slightly, her pale eyes, her thin figure, in a pink
 silk dressing-gown, give her an insubstantial quality in sharp
 contrast to Miss Scott's Roman grandeur. There is between the
 two women a mysterious tension, an atmosphere of something
 unspoken.*]

97

CORNELIA: I've already opened the mail.

GRACE: Anything of interest?

CORNELIA: A card from Thelma Peterson at Mayo's.

GRACE: Oh, how is Thelma?

CORNELIA: She says she's 'progressing nicely' whatever that indicates.

GRACE: Didn't she have something removed?

CORNELIA: Several things, I believe.

GRACE: Oh, here's the Fortnightly Review of Current Letters!

CORNELIA: Much to my astonishment. I thought I had cancelled my subscription to that publication.

GRACE: Really, Cornelia?

CORNELIA: Surely you remember. I cancelled my subscription immediately after the issue came out with that scurrilous attack on my cousin, Cecil Tutwiler Bates, the only dignified novelist the South has produced since Thomas Nelson Page.

GRACE: Oh, yes, I do remember. You wrote a furious letter of protest to the editor of the magazine and you received such a conciliatory reply from an associate editor named Caroline Something or Other that you were completely mollified and cancelled the cancellation!

CORNELIA: I have never been mollified by conciliatory replies, never completely and never even partially, and if I wrote to the editor in chief and was answered by an associate editor, my reaction to that piece of impertinence would hardly be what you call 'mollified'.

GRACE [*to change the subject*]: Oh, here's the new catalogue from the Gramophone Shoppe in Atlanta!

CORNELIA [*conceding a point*]: Yes, there it is.

GRACE: I see you've checked several items.

CORNELIA: I think we ought to build up our collection of Lieder.

GRACE: You've checked a Sibelius that we already have.

CORNELIA: It's getting a little bit scratchy. [*Inhales deeply and sighs, her look fastened upon the silent phone.*] – You'll also notice that I've checked a few operatic selections.

GRACE [*excitedly*]: Where, which ones, I don't see them!

CORNELIA: – Why are you so excited over the catalogue, dear?

GRACE: I adore phonograph records!

CORNELIA: I wish you adored them enough to put them back in their proper places in albums.

GRACE: Oh, here's the Vivaldi we wanted!

CORNELIA: Not 'we' dear. Just you.

GRACE: Not *you*, Cornelia?

CORNELIA: I think Vivaldi's a very thin shadow of Bach.

GRACE: – How strange that I should have the impression you –

[*Phone rings.*]

– Shall I answer?

CORNELIA: If you will be so kind.

GRACE [*lifting receiver*]: *Miss Scott's* residence! [*This announcement is made in a tone of reverence, as though mentioning a seat of holiness.*] Oh, no, this is Grace, but Cornelia is right by my side. [*Passing phone*] Esmeralda Hawkins.

CORNELIA [*grimly*]: I've been expecting her call. [*Into phone*] Hello, Esmeralda, my dear. I've been expecting your call. Now where are you calling me from? Of course I know that you're calling me from the meeting, *ça va sans dire, ma petite!* Ha ha! But from which phone in the house; there's two, you know, the one in the downstairs hall and the one in the chatelaine's boudoir where the ladies will probably be removing their wraps. Oh. You're on the downstairs', are you? Well, by this time I presume that practically all the Daughters have assembled. Now go upstairs and call me back from there so we can talk with a little more privacy, dear, as I want to make my position very clear before the meeting commences. Thank you dear. [*Hangs up. Looks grimly into space.*]

GRACE: – The – Confederate Daughters?

CORNELIA: Yes! They're holding the Annual Election today.

GRACE: Oh, how exciting! Why aren't you at the meeting?

CORNELIA: I preferred not to go.

GRACE: You preferred *not* to go?

CORNELIA: Yes, I preferred not to *go.* . . . [*She touches her chest, breathing heavily as if she had run upstairs.*]

GRACE: But it's the annual election of officers!

CORNELIA: Yes! I told you it was!

[GRACE *drops spoon.* CORNELIA *cries out and jumps a little.*]

GRACE: I'm so sorry! [*Rings bell for servant.*]

CORNELIA: Intrigue, intrigue and duplicity, revolt me so that I wouldn't be able to breathe in the same atmosphere!

[GRACE *rings bell louder.*]

Why are you ringing that bell? You know Lucinda's not here!

GRACE: I'm so sorry. Where has Lucinda gone?

CORNELIA [*in a hoarse whisper, barely audible*]: There's a big coloured funeral in town. [*Clears throat violently and repeats the statement.*]

GRACE: Oh, dear. You have that nervous laryngitis.

CORNELIA: No sleep, no sleep last night.

[*Phone screams at her elbow. She cries out and thrusts it from her as if it were on fire.*]

GRACE [*lifting phone*]: Miss Scott's residence. Oh. Just a moment please.

CORNELIA [*snatching phone*]: *Esmeralda, are you upstairs now?*

GRACE [*in a loud whisper*]: It isn't Esmeralda. It's Mrs C. C. Bright!

CORNELIA: One moment, one moment, one moment! [*Thrusts phone back at Grace with a glare of fury.*] How dare you put me on the line with that woman!

GRACE: Cornelia, I didn't, I was just going to ask if you –

CORNELIA: *Hush!* [*She springs back from table, glaring across it.*] – Now give me that phone. [GRACE *hands it to her. Coldly*] What can I do for you, please? No. I'm afraid that my garden will not be open to the Pilgrims this spring. I think the cultivation of gardens is an aesthetic hobby and not a competitive sport. Individual visitors will be welcome if they call in advance so that I can arrange for my gardener to show them around, but no bands of Pilgrims, not after the devastation my garden suffered last spring – Pilgrims coming with dogs – picking flowers and – You're

100

entirely welcome, yes, goodbye! [*Returns phone to Grace.*]

GRACE: I think the election would have been less of a strain if you'd gone to it, Cornelia.

CORNELIA: I don't know what you are talking about.

GRACE: Aren't you up for office?

CORNELIA: 'Up for office?' What is 'up for office'?

GRACE: Why, ha ha! – *running* for – something?

CORNELIA: – Have you ever known me to '*run*' for anything, Grace? Whenever I've held an office in a society or club it's been at the *insistence* of the members, because I really have an *aversion* to holding office. But this is a different thing, a different thing altogether. It's a test of something. You see, I have known for some time, now, that there is a little group, a *clique*, in the Daughters which is hostile to me!

GRACE: Oh, Cornelia, I'm sure you must be mistaken.

CORNELIA: No. There is a movement against me.

GRACE: A movement? A movement against you?

CORNELIA: An organized movement to keep me out of any important office.

GRACE: But haven't you always held some important office in the Chapter?

CORNELIA: I have never been *Regent* of it!

GRACE: Oh, you want to be *Regent*?

CORNELIA: No. You misunderstand me. I don't '*want*' to be Regent.

GRACE: Oh?

CORNELIA: I don't 'want' to be anything whatsoever. I simply want to break up this movement against me, and for that purpose I have rallied my forces.

GRACE: – Your – *forces*? [*Her lips twitch slightly as if she had a hysterical impulse to smile.*]

CORNELIA: Yes. I still have some friends in the Chapter who have resisted the movement.

GRACE: Oh?

CORNELIA: I have the solid support of all the older Board members.

GRACE: Why, then, I should think you'd have nothing to worry about!

CORNELIA: The Chapter has expanded too rapidly lately. Women have been admitted that couldn't get into a front pew at the Second Baptist Church! And that's the disgraceful truth. . . .

GRACE: – But since it's really a patriotic society . . .

CORNELIA: My dear Grace, there are two chapters of the Confederate Daughters in the city of Meridian. There is the Forrest Chapter, which is for social riff-raff, and there is *this* Chapter which was *supposed* to have a *little* bit of *distinction*! I'm not a snob. I'm nothing if not democratic. You know *that*! But –

[*Phone rings.* CORNELIA *reaches for it. Then pushes it to Grace.*]

GRACE: Miss Scott's residence! Oh, yes, yes, just a moment! [*Passes phone to Cornelia.*] It's Esmeralda Hawkins.

CORNELIA [*into phone*]: Are you upstairs now, dear? Well, I wondered. It took you so long to call back. Oh, but I thought you said the luncheon was over. Well, I'm glad that you fortified yourself with a bite to eat. What did the buffet consist of? Chicken *à la king*! Wouldn't you know it! That is so characteristic of poor Amelia! With bits of pimento and tiny mushrooms in it? What did the ladies counting their calories do! Nibbled around the edges? Oh, poor dears! – and afterwards I suppose there was lemon sherbet with lady-fingers? What, lime sherbet! And *no* lady-fingers? *What a departure!* What a *shocking* apostasy! I'm quite stunned! Ho ho ho . . . [*Reaches shakily for cup.*] – Now what's going on? Discussing the Civil Rights Programme? Then they won't take the vote for at least half an hour! – Now, Esmeralda, I *do* hope that you understand my position clearly. I don't wish to hold any office in the Chapter unless it's by acclamation. You know what that means, don't you? It's a parliamentary term. It means when someone is desired for an office so unanimously that no vote has to be taken. In other words, elected automatically, simply by nomination, unopposed. Yes, my dear; it's just as simple as that. I have served as Treasurer for three terms, twice as Secretary, once as Chaplain – and what a dreary office that was with those long-drawn prayers for the Confederate dead! – Altogether I've served on the Board for, let's see, fourteen years! – Well, now, my dear, the point is simply this, If the Daughters feel that I have demonstrated my capabilities and loyalty strongly enough that I should simply be named as Regent without a vote being taken – by unanimous acclamation! – why, then, of course I would feel obliged to accept.... [*Her voice trembles with emotion.*] – But if, on the other hand, the – uh – *clique*! – and you know the ones I mean! – is bold enough to propose someone else for the office – Do you understand my position? In that eventuality, hard as it is to imagine, – I prefer to bow out of the picture entirely! – The moment another nomination is made and seconded, my own must be withdrawn, at once, unconditionally! Is that quite understood, Esmeralda? Then good! Go back downstairs to the meeting. Digest your chicken *à la king*, my dear, and call me again on the upstairs phone as soon as there's something to tell me.

[*Hangs up and stares grimly into space.* GRACE *lifts a section of grapefruit on a tiny silver fork.*]

GRACE: They haven't had it yet?

CORNELIA: Had what, dear?

GRACE: The election!

CORNELIA: No, not yet. It seems to be – imminent, though. . . .

GRACE: Cornelia, why don't you think about something else until it's over!

CORNELIA: What makes you think that I am nervous about it?

GRACE: You're – you're *breathing* so fast!

CORNELIA: I didn't sleep well last night. You were prowling about the house with that stitch in your side.

GRACE: I *am* so sorry. You know it's nothing. A muscular contraction that comes from strain.

CORNELIA: What strain does it come from, Grace?

GRACE: What strain? [*Utters a faint, perplexed laugh.*] Why! – I don't know....

CORNELIA: The strain of *what*? Would you like *me* to tell you?

GRACE: – Excuse me, I – [*Rises.*]

CORNELIA [*sharply*]: Where are you going?

GRACE: Upstairs for a moment! I just remembered I should have taken my drops of belladonna!

CORNELIA: It does no good *after* eating.

GRACE: I suppose that's right. It doesn't.

CORNELIA: But you want to escape?

GRACE: Of course not. . . .

CORNELIA: Several times lately you've rushed away from me as if I'd suddenly threatened you with a knife.

GRACE: Cornelia! – I've been – jumpy!

CORNELIA: It's always when something is almost – *spoken* – between us!

GRACE: – I hate to see you so agitated over the outcome of a silly club-woman's election!

CORNELIA: I'm not talking about the Daughters. I'm not even thinking about them, I'm –

GRACE: I wish you'd dismiss it completely from your mind. Now would be a good time to play some records. Let me put a symphony on the machine!

CORNELIA: No.

GRACE: How about the Bach for piano and strings! The one we received for Christmas from Jessie and Gay?

CORNELIA: No, I said, No, I said, No!

GRACE: – Something very light and quiet, then! The old French madrigals, maybe?

CORNELIA: Anything to avoid a talk between us? Anything to evade a conversation, especially when the servant is not in the house?

GRACE: Oh, here it is! This is just the thing! [*She has started the phonograph. Landowska playing a harpsichord selection. The phonograph is at the edge of the lighted area or just outside it.* CORNELIA *stares grimly as* GRACE *resumes her seat with an affection of enchantment, clasping her hands and closing her eyes. Enchanted*] Oh, how it smooths things over, how sweet, and gentle, and – pure. . . .

CORNELIA: – Yes! And completely dishonest!

GRACE: Music? Dishonest?

CORNELIA: Completely! It 'smooths things over' instead of –
speaking them out . . .

GRACE: 'Music hath charms to soothe the savage breast.'

CORNELIA: Yes, oh, yes. If the savage breast permits it.

GRACE: Oh, sublime – sublime. . . .

CORNELIA [*grudgingly*]: Landowska is an artist of rare pre-
cision.

GRACE [*ecstatically*]: And such a noble face, a profile as fine
and strong as Edith Sitwell's. After this we'll play Edith
Sitwell's *Façade*. 'Jane, Jane, tall as a crane, the morning
light creaks down again. . . .'

CORNELIA: Dearest, isn't there something you've failed to
notice?

GRACE: – Where?

CORNELIA: Right under your nose.

GRACE: Oh! You mean my flower?

CORNELIA: Yes! I mean your rose!

GRACE: Of course I noticed my rose. The moment I came in
the room I saw it here!

CORNELIA: You made no allusion to it.

GRACE: I would have, but you were so concerned over the
meeting.

CORNELIA: I'm not concerned over the meeting.

GRACE: – Whom do I have to thank for this lovely rose? My
gracious employer?

CORNELIA: You will find fourteen others on your desk in the
library when you go in to take care of the correspondence.

GRACE: Fourteen other roses?

CORNELIA: A total of fifteen!

GRACE: How wonderful! – Why fifteen?

CORNELIA: How long have you been here, dearest? How
long have you made this house a house of roses?

GRACE: – What a nice way to put it! Why, of course! I've
been your secretary for fifteen years!

CORNELIA: Fifteen years my companion! A rose for every
year, a year for every rose!

GRACE: What a charming sort of a way to – observe the –
occasion. . . .

CORNELIA: First I thought 'Pearls' and then I thought; No, roses. But perhaps I should have given you something golden, ha ha! – Silence is golden, they say!

GRACE: Oh, dear, that stupid machine is playing the same record over!

CORNELIA: Let it, let it, I like it!

GRACE: Just let me –

CORNELIA: Sit down!! – It was fifteen years ago this very morning, on the sixth day of November, that someone very sweet and gentle and silent! – a shy, little, quiet little widow! – arrived for the first time at Seven Edgewater Drive. The season was autumn. I had been raking dead leaves over the rose-bushes to protect them from frost when I heard footsteps on the gravel – light, quick, delicate footsteps like spring coming in the middle of autumn – and looked up, and sure enough, there spring was! A little person so thin that light shone through her as if she were made of the silk of a white parasol!

[GRACE *utters a short, startled laugh.*]

[*Harshly; wounded*] – Why did you laugh? Why did you laugh like that?

GRACE: It sounded – ha ha! – it sounded like the first paragraph of a woman's magazine story.

CORNELIA: – What a cutting remark!

GRACE: I didn't mean it that way, I –

CORNELIA: What other way could you mean it!

GRACE: Cornelia, you know how I am! I'm always a little embarrassed by sentiment, aren't I?

CORNELIA: Yes. Frightened of anything that betrays some feeling!

GRACE: People who don't know you well, nearly all people we know, would be astounded to hear you, Cornelia Scott, that grave and dignified lady, expressing herself in such a lyrical manner!

CORNELIA: People who don't know me well are everybody! Yes, I think even *you*!

GRACE: Cornelia, you must admit that sentiment isn't like you!

CORNELIA: *Is nothing like me but silence?*
[*Clock ticks loudly.*]
Am I sentenced to silence for a lifetime?

GRACE: – It's just not like you to –

CORNELIA: Not like me. Not like me. What do you know
what's like me or not like me!

GRACE: You may deny it, Cornelia, as much as you please,
but it's evident to me that you are completely unstrung by
your anxieties over the Confederate Daughters' election!

CORNELIA: – Another thinly veiled insult?

GRACE: Oh, Cornelia, please!

CORNELIA [*imitating her gesture*]: 'Oh, Cornelia, please!!'

GRACE: If I've said anything wrong, I beg your pardon, I
offer my very humble apologies for it.

CORNELIA: I don't want apologies from you.
[*Strained silence. Clock ticks. Suddenly* GRACE *reaches across
to touch the veined jewelled hand of Miss Scott.* CORNELIA
snatches her own hand away as though the touch had burned her.]

GRACE: Thank you for the roses.

CORNELIA: I don't want thanks from you either. All that I
want is a little return of affection – not much, but sometimes
a little!

GRACE: You have that always, Cornelia.

CORNELIA: And one thing more: a little outspokenness, too.

GRACE: – Outspokenness?

CORNELIA: Yes, outspokenness, if that's not too much to ask
from such a proud young lady!

GRACE [*rising from table*]: I am not proud and I am not young,
Cornelia.

CORNELIA: Sit down. Don't leave the table.

GRACE: Is that an order?

CORNELIA: I don't give orders to you, I make requests!

GRACE: Sometimes the requests of an employer are hard to
distinguish from orders. [*She sits down.*]

CORNELIA: Please turn off the victrola.
[GRACE *rises and stops the machine.*]
Grace! – Don't you feel there's – *something unspoken* between
?

GRACE: No. No, I don't.

CORNELIA: I do. I've felt for a long time something unspoken between us.

GRACE: – Don't you think there is always something unspoken between two people?

CORNELIA: I see no reason for it.

GRACE: But don't a great many things exist without reason?

CORNELIA: Let's not turn this into a metaphysical discussion.

GRACE: All right. But you mystify me.

CORNELIA: It's very simple. It's just that I feel that there's something unspoken between us that ought to be spoken. – – Why are you looking at me like that?

GRACE: How am I looking at you?

CORNELIA: With positive terror!

GRACE: Cornelia!

CORNELIA: You are, you are, but I'm not going to be shut up!

GRACE: Go on, continue, please, do!

CORNELIA: I'm going to, I will, I will, I –

[*Phone rings.* GRACE *reaches for it.*]

No, no, no, let it ring!

[*It goes on ringing.*]

Take it off the hook!

GRACE: Do just let me –

CORNELIA: Off the hook I told you!

[GRACE *takes phone off hook. A voice says; 'Hello? Hello? Hello? Hello?'*]

GRACE [*suddenly sobbing*]: I can't stand it!

CORNELIA: Be STILL! *Someone can hear you!*

Voice: Hello? Hello? Cornelia? Cornelia Scott?

[CORNELIA *seizes phone and slams it back into cradle.*]

CORNELIA: Now stop that! Stop that silly little female trick!

GRACE: You say there's something unspoken. Maybe there is. I don't know. But I do know some things are better left unspoken. Also I know that when a silence between two people has gone on for a long time it's like a wall that's impenetrable between them! Maybe between us there is such a wall. One that's impenetrable. Or maybe *you* can break it. I know I can't. I can't even attempt to. You're the strong one of us two, and surely you know it. – Both of us have turned grey! – But not the same kind of grey. In that velvet dressing-gown you look like the Emperor Tiberius! – In his imperial toga! – Your hair and your eyes are both the colour of iron! Iron-grey. Invincible-looking! People are nearly all somewhat – frightened of you. They feel your force and they admire you for it. They come to you here for opinions on this or that. What plays are good on Broadway this season, what books are worth reading and what books are trash and what – what records are valuable and – what is the proper attitude toward – Bills in Congress! – Oh, you're a fountain of wisdom! – And in addition to that, you have your – *wealth*! Yes, you have your – *fortune*! – All of your real-estate holdings, your blue-chip stocks, your – bonds, your – mansion on Edgewater Drive, your – shy little – secretary, your – fabulous gardens that Pilgrims cannot go into. . . .

CORNELIA: Oh, yes, now you are speaking, now you are speaking at last! Go on, please go on speaking.

GRACE: I am – very – different! – Also turning grey, but my grey is different. Not iron, like yours, not imperial, Cornelia, but grey, yes, grey, the – colour of a – *cobweb*. . . . [*She starts the record again, very softly.*] – Something white getting soiled, the grey of something forgotten.

    [*Phone rings again. Neither of them seems to notice it.*]

– And that being the case, that being the difference between our two kinds of grey, yours and mine – You mustn't expect me to give bold answers to questions that make the house shake with silence! To speak out things that are fifteen years unspoken!? – That long a time can make a silence a wall that nothing less than dynamite could break through and – [*Picks up phone*] I'm not strong enough, bold enough, I'm not –

CORNELIA [*fiercely*]: You're speaking into the phone!

GRACE [*into phone*]: Hello? Oh, yes, she's here. It's Esmeralda Hawkins.

CORNELIA [*snatches the phone*]: What is it, Esmeralda? What are you saying? Is the room full of women? Such a babble of voices! What are you trying to tell me? Have they held the election already? What, what, what? Oh, this is maddening! I can't hear a word that you're saying. It sounds like the Fourth of July, a great celebration! Ha ha! Now try once more with your mouth closer to the phone! What, what? Would I be willing to what? You can't be serious! Are you out of your mind? [*To Grace in a panicky voice*] She wants to know if I would be willing to serve as *Vice*-Regent! [*Back into phone*] Esmeralda! Will you listen to me? What's going on! Are there some fresh defections? How does it look? Why did you call me again before the vote? Louder, please speak louder, and cup your mouth to the phone in case they're eavesdropping! Who asked if I would accept the Vice-Regency, dear? Oh, Mrs Colby, of course! – that treacherous witch! – *Esmeralda!* Listen! I – WILL ACCEPT – NO OFFICE – EXCEPT – THE HIGHEST! Did you understand that? I – WILL ACCEPT NO OFFICE EXCEPT – ESMERALDA! [*Drops phone into cradle.*]

GRACE: – Have they held the election?

CORNELIA [*dazed*]: What? – No, there's a five-minute recess before the election begins. . . .

GRACE: – Things are not going well?

CORNELIA: 'Would you accept the Vice-Regency' she asked me, 'if for some reason they don't elect you Regent?' – Then she hung up as if somebody had snatched the phone away from her, or the house had – caught fire!

GRACE: You shouted so I think she must have been frightened.

CORNELIA: – Whom can you trust in this world, whom can you ever rely on?

GRACE: I think perhaps you should have gone to the meeting.

CORNELIA: I think my not being there is much more pointed.

GRACE [*rising again*]: May I be excused, now?

CORNELIA: No! Stay here!

GRACE: If that is just a request, I –

CORNELIA: That's an order!

[GRACE *sits down and closes her eyes.*]

CORNELIA: When you first came to this house – do you know I didn't expect you?

GRACE: Oh, but, Cornelia, you'd invited me here.

CORNELIA: We hardly knew each other.

GRACE: We'd met the summer before, when Ralph was –

CORNELIA: – Living! Yes, we met at Sewanee, where he was a summer instructor.

GRACE: – He was already ill.

CORNELIA: I thought what a pity that lovely, delicate girl hasn't found someone she could lean on, who could protect her! And two months later I heard through Clarabelle Drake that he was dead. . . .

GRACE: You wrote me such a sweet letter, saying how lonely you were since the loss of your mother and urging me to rest here till the shock was over. You seemed to understand how badly I needed to withdraw for a while from – old associations. I hesitated to come. I didn't until you wrote me a second letter. . . .

CORNELIA: – After I received yours. You wanted urging.

GRACE: I wanted to be quite sure I was really wanted! I only came intending to stay a few weeks. I was so afraid that I would outstay my welcome!

CORNELIA: How blind of you not to see how desperately I wanted to keep you here for ever!

GRACE: Oh, I did see that you –

[*Phone rings. She snatches it up.*]

Miss Scott's residence! – Yes, she's here.

CORNELIA [*snatches it finally up*]: – Cornelia Scott speaking! Oh. It's you, Esmeralda! Well, how did it come out? – *I don't believe you! I simply don't believe you.* . . .

[GRACE *sits down quietly at the table.*]

– MRS HORNSBY ELECTED? Well, there's a dark horse for you! Less than a year in the Chapter. . . . Did you – nominate me? – Oh – I see! But I told you to withdraw my name if – No, no, no, don't explain, it doesn't matter, I have too much already. You know I am going into the Daughters of the Barons of Runnymede! Yes; it's been established, I have a direct line to the Earl of – No, it's been straightened out, a clear line is established, and then, of course, I am also eligible for the Colonial Dames and for the Huguenot Society, and what with all my other activities and so forth, why, I couldn't *possibly* have taken it on if they'd – *wanted* ... Of course I'm going to resign from the local Chapter! Oh, yes, I am! My secretary is sitting right here by me. She has her pencil, her notebook! I'm going to dictate my letter of resignation from the local Chapter the moment that I hang up on this conversation. Oh, no, no, no, I'm not mad, not outraged, at all. I'm just a little – ha ha! – a little – amused. ... MRS HORNSBY? Nothing succeeds like mediocrity, does it?! Thanks and goodbye, Esmeralda.

[*Hangs up; stunned.* GRACE *rises.*]

GRACE: Notebook and pencil?

CORNELIA: Yes. Notebook and pencil.... – I have to – dictate a letter ...

[GRACE *leaves the table. Just at the edge of the lighted area, she turns to glance at Cornelia's rigid shoulders, and a slight, equivocal smile appears momentarily on her face; not quite malicious, but not really sympathetic. Then she crosses out of the light. A moment later her voice comes from the outer dark.*]

GRACE: *What lovely roses! One for every year!*

CURTAIN

SUDDENLY LAST SUMMER

SCENE ONE

The set may be as unrealistic as the decor of a dramatic ballet. It represents part of a mansion of Victorian Gothic style in the Garden District of New Orleans on a late afternoon, between late summer and early fall. The interior is blended with a fantastic garden which is more like a tropical jungle, or forest, in the prehistoric age of giant fern-forests when living creatures had flippers turning to limbs and scales to skin. The colours of this jungle-garden are violent, especially since it is steaming with heat after rain. There are massive tree-flowers that suggest organs of a body, torn out, still glistening with undried blood; there are harsh cries and sibilant hissings and thrashing sounds in the garden as if it were inhabited by beasts, serpents, and birds, all of savage nature....

[*The jungle tumult continues a few moments after the curtain rises; then subsides into relative quiet, which is occasionally broken by a new outburst.*

A lady enters with the assistance of a silver-knobbed cane. She has light orange or pink hair and wears a lavender lace dress, and over her withered bosom is pinned a starfish of diamonds.

She is followed by a young blond DOCTOR, *all in white, glacially brilliant, very, very good-looking, and the old lady's manner and eloquence indicate her undeliberate response to his icy charm.*]

MRS VENABLE: Yes, this was Sebastian's garden. The Latin names of the plants were printed on tags attached to them but the print's fading out. Those ones there – [*She draws a deep breath.*] – are the oldest plants on earth, survivors from the age of the giant fern-forests. Of course in this semi-tropical climate – [*She takes another deep breath.*] – some of the rarest plants, such as the Venus flytrap – you know what this is, Doctor? The Venus flytrap?

DOCTOR: An insectivorous plant?

MRS VENABLE: Yes, it feeds on insects. It has to be kept under glass from early fall to late spring and when it went under glass, my son, Sebastian, had to provide it with fruit flies flown in at great expense from a Florida laboratory that used fruit flies for experiments in genetics. Well, I can't do that, Doctor. [*She takes a deep breath.*] I can't, I just can't do it! It's not the expense but the –

DOCTOR: Effort.

MRS VENABLE: Yes. So goodbye, Venus flytrap! – like so much else ... Whew! ... [*She draws breath.*] – I don't know why, but – ! I already feel I can lean on your shoulder, Doctor – Cu? – Cu?

DOCTOR: Cu-kro-wicz. It's a Polish word that means sugar, so let's make it simple and call me Doctor Sugar. [*He returns her smile.*]

MRS VENABLE: Well, now, Doctor Sugar, you've seen Sebastian's garden.

[*They are advancing slowly to the patio area.*]

DOCTOR: It's like a well-groomed jungle. . . .

MRS VENABLE: That's how he meant it to be, nothing was accidental, everything was planned and designed in Sebastian's life and his – [*She dabs her forehead with her handkerchief, which she had taken from her reticule.*] – work!

DOCTOR: What was your son's work, Mrs Venable? – besides this garden?

MRS VENABLE: As many times as I've had to answer that question! D'you know it still shocks me a little? – to realize that Sebastian Venable the poet is still unknown outside of a small coterie of friends, including his mother.

DOCTOR: Oh.

MRS VENABLE: You see, strictly speaking, his *life* was his occupation.

DOCTOR: I see.

MRS VENABLE: No, you *don't* see, yet, but before I'm through, you will. – Sebastian was a poet? That's what I meant when I said his life was his work because the work of a poet is the life of a poet, and – vice versa, the life of a poet is the work of a poet, I mean you can't separate them, I mean – well, for instance, a salesman's work is one thing and his life is

114

another – or can be. The same thing's true of – doctor, lawyer, merchant, *thief*! – But a poet's life is his work and his work is his life in a special sense because – oh, I've already talked myself breathless and dizzy.

[*The* DOCTOR *offers his arm.*]

Thank you.

DOCTOR: Mrs Venable, did your doctor okay this thing?

MRS VENABLE [*breathless*]: What thing?

DOCTOR: Your meeting this girl that you think is responsible for your son's death?

MRS VENABLE: I've waited months to face her because I couldn't get to St Mary's to face her – I've had her brought here to my house. I won't collapse! She'll collapse! I mean her lies will collapse – not my truth – not the truth.... *Forward march, Doctor Sugar!*

[*He conducts her slowly to the patio.*]

Ah, we've *made* it, *ha ha!* I didn't know that I was so weak on my pins! Sit down, Doctor. I'm not afraid of using every last ounce and inch of my little, left-over strength in doing just what I'm doing. I'm devoting all that's left of my life, Doctor, to the defence of a dead poet's reputation. Sebastian had no public name as a poet, he didn't want one, he refused to have one. He *dreaded, abhorred*! – false values that come from being publicly known, from fame, from personal – exploitation.... Oh, he'd say to me: 'Violet? Mother? – You're going to outlive me!!'

DOCTOR: What made him think that?

MRS VENABLE: Poets are always clairvoyant! – And he had rheumatic fever when he was fifteen and it affected a heart-valve and he wouldn't stay off horses and out of water and so forth.... 'Violet? Mother? You're going to live longer than me, and then, when I'm gone, it will be yours, in your hands, to do whatever you please with!' – Meaning, of course, his future recognition! – That he *did* want, he wanted it after his death when it couldn't disturb him; then he did want to offer his work to the world. All right. Have I made my point, Doctor? Well, here is my son's work, Doctor, here's his life going *on*!

[*She lifts a thin gilt-edged volume from the patio table as if elevating the Host before the altar. Its gold leaf and lettering catch the afternoon sun. It says* Poem of Summer. *Her face suddenly has a different look, the look of a visionary, an exalted* religieuse. *At the same instant a bird sings clearly and purely in the garden and the old lady seems to be almost young for a moment.*]

DOCTOR [*reading the title*]: *Poem of Summer?*

MRS VENABLE: *Poem of Summer,* and the date of the summer, there are twenty-five of them, he wrote one poem a year which he printed himself on an eighteenth-century hand-press at his – *atelier* in the – French – Quarter – so no one but he could see it. . . .

[*She seems dizzy for a moment.*]

DOCTOR: He wrote one poem a year?

MRS VENABLE: One for each summer that we travelled together. The other nine months of the year were really only a preparation.

DOCTOR: Nine months?

MRS VENABLE: The length of a pregnancy, yes. . . .

DOCTOR: The poem was hard to deliver?

MRS VENABLE: Yes, even with me! *Without* me, *impossible,* Doctor! – he wrote no poem last summer.

DOCTOR: He died last summer?

MRS VENABLE: Without me he died last summer, that was his last summer's poem. [*She staggers; he assists her toward a chair. She catches her breath with difficulty.*] One long-ago summer – now, why am I thinking of this? – my son, Sebastian, said, 'Mother? – Listen to this!' – He read me Herman Melville's description of the Encantadas, the Galapagos Islands. Quote – take five and twenty heaps of cinders dumped here and there in an outside city lot. Imagine some of them magnified into mountains, and the vacant lot, the sea. And you'll have a fit idea of the general aspect of the Encantadas, the Enchanted Isles – extinct volcanoes, looking much as the world at large might look – after a last conflagration – end quote. He read me that description and said that we had to go there. And so we did go there that summer on a chartered boat a four-masted schooner, as close as possible to the sort of a boat that Melville must have sailed on. . . . We saw the Encantadas, but on the Encantadas we saw something Melville *hadn't* written about. We saw the great sea-turtles crawl up out of the sea for their annual egg-laying. . . . Once a year the female of the sea-turtle crawls up out of the equatorial sea on to the blazing sand-beach of a volcanic island to dig a pit in the sand and deposit her eggs there. It's a long and dreadful thing, the depositing of the eggs in the sand-pits, and when it's finished the exhausted female turtle crawls back to the sea half-dead. She never sees her offspring, but we did. Sebastian knew exactly when the sea-turtle eggs would be hatched out and we returned in time for it. . . .

DOCTOR: You went back to the – ?

MRS VENABLE: Terrible Encantadas, those heaps of extinct volcanoes, in time to witness the hatching of the sea-turtles and their desperate flight to the sea!

[*There is a sound of harsh bird-cries in the air. She looks up.*]

– The narrow beach, the colour of caviar, was all in motion! But the sky was in motion, too. . . .

DOCTOR: The sky was in motion, too?

MRS VENABLE: – Full of flesh-eating birds and the noise of the birds, the horrible savage cries of the –

DOCTOR: Carnivorous birds?

MRS VENABLE: Over the narrow black heath of the Encantadas as the just-hatched sea-turtles scrambled out of the sand-pits and started their race to the sea. . . .

DOCTOR: Race to the sea?

MRS VENABLE: To escape the flesh-eating birds that made the sky almost as black as the beach!

[*She gazes up again; we hear the wild, ravenous, harsh cries of the birds. The sound comes in rhythmic waves like a savage chant.*]

And the sand all alive, all alive, as the hatched sea-turtles made their dash for the sea, while the birds hovered and swooped to attack and hovered and – swooped to attack! They were diving down on the hatched sea-turtles, turning sides open and rending and eating their flesh. Sebastian guessed that possibly only a hundredth of one per cent of their number would escape to the sea. . . .

DOCTOR: What was it about this that fascinated your son?

MRS VENABLE: My son was looking for – [*She stops short with a slight gasp.*] – Let's just say he was interested in sea-turtles!

DOCTOR: That isn't what you started to say.

MRS VENABLE: I stopped myself just in time.

DOCTOR: Say what you started to say.

MRS VENABLE: I started to say that my son was looking for God and I stopped myself because I thought you'd think 'Oh, a pretentious young crackpot!' – which Sebastian was *not*!

DOCTOR: Mrs Venable, doctors look for God, too.

MRS VENABLE: Oh?

DOCTOR: I think they have to look harder for him than priests since they don't have the help of such well-known guide-books and well-organized expeditions as the priests have with their scriptures and – churches. . . .

MRS VENABLE: You mean they go on a solitary safari like a poet?

DOCTOR: Yes. Some do. I do.

MRS VENABLE: I believe, I *believe* you! [*She laughs, startled.*]

DOCTOR: Let me tell you something – the first operation I performed at Lion's View. – You can imagine how anxious and nervous I was about the outcome.

MRS VENABLE: Yes.

DOCTOR: The patient was a young girl regarded as hopeless and put in the Drum –

MRS VENABLE: Yes.

DOCTOR: The name for the violent ward at Lion's View because it looks like the inside of a drum with very bright lights burning all day and all night. – So the attendants can see any change of expression or movement among the inmates in time to grab them if they're about to attack. After the operation I stayed with the girl, as if I'd delivered a child that might stop breathing. – When they finally wheeled her out of the surgery, I still stayed with her. I walked along by the rolling table holding on to her hand – with my heart in my throat.

[*We hear faint music.*]

– It was a nice afternoon, as fair as this one. And the moment we wheeled her outside, she whispered something, she whispered: 'Oh, how blue the sky is!' – And I felt proud, I felt proud and relieved because up till then her speech, everything that she'd babbled, was a torrent of obscenities!

MRS VENABLE: Yes, well, now, I can tell you without any hesitation that my son *was* looking for God, I mean for a clear image of Him. He spent that whole blazing equatorial day in the crow's-nest of the schooner watching this thing on the beach till it was too dark to see it, and when he came down the rigging he said 'Well, now I've seen Him!', and he meant God. – And for several weeks after that he had a fever, he was delirious with it –

[*The Encantadas music then fades in again, briefly, at a lower level, a whisper.*]

DOCTOR: I can see how he *might* be, I think he *would* be disturbed if he thought he'd seen God's image, an equation of God, in that spectacle you watched in the Encantadas: creatures of the air hovering over and swooping down to devour creatures of the sea that had had the bad luck to be hatched on land and weren't able to scramble back into the sea fast enough to escape that massacre you witnessed, yes, I can see how such a spectacle could be equated with a good deal of – *experience, existence!* – but not with *God!* Can *you?*

MRS VENABLE: Dr Sugar, I'm a reasonably loyal member of the Protestant Episcopal Church, but I understood what he meant.

DOCTOR: Did he mean we must rise above God?

MRS VENABLE: He meant that God shows a savage face to people and shouts some fierce things at them, it's all we see or hear of Him. Isn't it all we ever really see and hear of Him, now? – Nobody seems to know why....

[*Music fades out again.*]

Shall I go on from there?

DOCTOR: Yes, do.

MRS VENABLE: Well, next? – India – China –

[MISS FOXHILL *appears with the medicine.* MRS VENABLE *sees her.*]

FOXHILL: Mrs Venable.

MRS VENABLE: Oh, God – elixir of – [*She takes the glass.*] Isn't it kind of the drugstore to keep me alive. Where was I, Doctor?

DOCTOR: In the Himalayas.

MRS VENABLE: Oh yes, that long-ago summer.... In the Himalayas he almost entered a Buddhist monastery, had gone so far as to shave his head and eat just rice out of a wood bowl on a grass mat. He'd promised those sly Buddhist monks that he would give up the world and himself and all his worldly possessions to their mendicant order. – Well, I cabled his father, 'For God's sake notify bank to freeze Sebastian's accounts!' – I got back this cable from my late husband's lawyer: 'Mr Venable critically ill Stop Wants you Stop Needs you Stop Immediate return advised most strongly Stop Cable time of arrival....'

DOCTOR: Did you go back to your husband?

MRS VENABLE: I made the hardest decision of my life. I stayed with my son. I got him through that crisis too. In less than a month he got up off the filthy grass mat and threw the rice bowl away – and booked us into Shepheard's Hotel in Cairo and the Ritz in Paris – And from then on, oh, we – still lived in a – world of light and shadow.... [*She turns vaguely with empty glass. He rises and takes it from her.*] But the shadow was almost as luminous as the light.

DOCTOR: Don't you want to sit down now?

MRS VENABLE: Yes, indeed I do, before I fall down.

[*He assists her into wheelchair.*]

– Are your hind-legs still on you?

DOCTOR [*still concerned over her agitation*]: – My what? Oh – hind-legs! – Yes ...

MRS VENABLE: Well, then you're not a donkey, you're certainly not a donkey because I've been talking the hind-legs off a donkey – several donkeys.... But I had to make it clear to you that the world lost a great deal too when I lost my son last summer.... You would have liked my son; he would have been charmed by you. My son, Sebastian, was not a family snob or a money snob, but he was a snob, all right. He was a snob about personal charm in people, he insisted upon good looks in people around him, and, oh, he had a perfect little court of young and beautiful people around him always, wherever he was, here in New *Orleans* or New York or on the Riviera or in Paris and Venice, he always had a little entourage of the beautiful and the talented and the young!

DOCTOR: Your son was young, Mrs Venable?

MRS VENABLE: Both of us were young, and stayed young, Doctor.

DOCTOR: Could I see a photograph of your son, Mrs Venable?

MRS VENABLE: Yes, indeed you could, Doctor. I'm glad that you asked to see one. I'm going to show you not one photograph but two. Here. Here is my son, Sebastian, in a Renaissance page-boy's costume at a masked ball in Cannes. Here is my son, Sebastian, in the same costume at a masked ball in Venice. These two pictures were taken twenty years apart. Now which is the older one, Doctor?

DOCTOR: This photograph looks older.

MRS VENABLE: The photograph looks older, but not the subject. It takes character to refuse to grow old, Doctor – successfully to refuse to. It calls for discipline, abstention. One cocktail before dinner, not two, four, six – a single lean chop and lime juice on a salad in restaurants famed for rich dishes.

[FOXHILL *comes from the house*.]

FOXHILL: Mrs Venable, Miss Holly's mother and brother are –

[*Simultaneously* MRS HOLLY *and* GEORGE *appear in the window*.]

GEORGE: Hi, Aunt Vi!

MRS HOLLY: Violet dear, we're here.

FOXHILL: They're here.

MRS VENABLE: Wait upstairs in my upstairs living-room for

me. [*To Miss Foxhill*] Get them upstairs. I don't want them at that window during this talk. [*To the Doctor*] Let's get away from the window.

[*He wheels her to stage centre.*]

DOCTOR: Mrs Venable? Did your son have a – well – what kind of a *personal*, well, *private* life did –

MRS VENABLE: That's a question I wanted you to ask me.

DOCTOR: Why?

MRS VENABLE: I haven't heard the girl's story except indirectly in a watered-down version, being too ill to go to hear it directly, but I've gathered enough to know that it's a hideous attack on my son's moral character which, being dead, he can't defend himself from. I have to be the defender. Now. Sit down. Listen to me....

[*The DOCTOR sits.*]

... before you hear whatever you're going to hear from the girl when she gets here. My son, Sebastian, was chaste. Not c-h-a-s-e-d! Oh, he was chased in that way of spelling it, too, we had to be very fleet-footed I can tell you, with his looks and his charm, to keep ahead of pursuers, every kind of pursuer! – I mean he was c-h-a-s-t-e! – Chaste....

DOCTOR: I understood what you meant, Mrs Venable.

MRS VENABLE: And you *believe* me, don't you?

DOCTOR: Yes, but –

MRS VENABLE: But *what*?

DOCTOR: Chastity at – what age was your son last summer?

MRS VENABLE: *Forty*, maybe. We really didn't count birthdays....

DOCTOR: He lived a celibate life?

MRS VENABLE: As strictly as if he'd *vowed* to! This sounds like vanity, Doctor, but really I was actually the only one in his life that satisfied the demands he made of people. Time after time my son would let people go, dismiss them! – because their, their, their! – *attitude* toward him was –

DOCTOR: Not as pure as –

MRS VENABLE: My son, Sebastian, demanded! We were a famous couple. People didn't speak of Sebastian and his mother or Mrs Venable and her son, they said, 'Sebastian and Violet, Violet and Sebastian are staying at the Lido, they're at the Ritz in Madrid. Sebastian and Violet, Violet and Sebastian have taken a house at Biarritz for the season,' and every appearance, every time we appeared, attention was centred on *us! – everyone else! Eclipsed!* Vanity? Ohhhh, no, Doctor, you can't call it that –

DOCTOR: I didn't call it that.

MRS VENABLE: – It wasn't *folie de grandeur*, it was grandeur.

DOCTOR: I see.

MRS VENABLE: An attitude toward life that's hardly been known in the world since the great Renaissance princes were crowded out of their palaces and gardens by successful shopkeepers!

DOCTOR: I see.

MRS VENABLE: Most people's lives – what are they but trails of debris, each day more debris, more debris, long, long trails of debris with nothing to clean it all up but, finally, death. . . .

[*We hear lyric music.*]

My son, Sebastian, and I constructed our days, each day, we would – carve out each day of our lives like a piece of sculpture. – Yes, we left behind us a trail of days like a gallery of sculpture! But, last summer –

[*Pause: the music continues.*]

I can't forgive him for it, not even now that he's paid for it with his life! – he let in this – *vandal!* This –

DOCTOR: The girl that – ?

MRS VENABLE: That you're going to meet here this afternoon! Yes. He admitted this vandal and with her tongue for a hatchet she's gone about smashing our legend, the memory of –

DOCTOR: Mrs Venable, what do you think is her reason?

MRS VENABLE: Lunatics don't have reason!

DOCTOR: I mean, what do you think is her – motive?

MRS VENABLE: What a question! – We put the bread in her mouth and the clothes on her back. People that like you for that or even forgive you for it are, are – *hen's teeth*, Doctor. The role of the benefactor is worse than thankless, it's the role of a victim, Doctor, a sacrificial victim, yes, they want your blood, Doctor, they want your blood on the altar steps of their *outraged, outrageous* egos!

DOCTOR: Oh. You mean she resented the –

MRS VENABLE: Loathed! – They can't shut her up at St Mary's.

DOCTOR: I thought she'd been there for months.

MRS VENABLE: I mean keep her *still* there. She *babbles*! They couldn't shut her up in Cabeza de Lobo or at the clinic in Paris – she babbled, babbled! – smashing my son's reputation. – On the *Berengaria* bringing her back to the States she broke out of the state room and babbled, babbled; even at the airport when she was flown down here, she babbled a bit of her story before they could whisk her into an ambulance to St Mary's. This is a reticule, Doctor. [*She raises a cloth bag.*] A catch-all, carry-all bag for an elderly lady which I turned into last summer.... Will you open it for me, my hands are stiff, and fish out some cigarettes and a cigarette holder.

[*He does.*]

DOCTOR: I don't have matches.

MRS VENABLE: I think there's a table-lighter on the table.

DOCTOR: Yes, there is. [*He lights it, it flames up high.*] My Lord, what a torch!

MRS VENABLE [*with a sudden, sweet smile*]: 'So shines a good deed in a naughty world,' Doctor – Sugar....

[*Pause. A bird sings sweetly in the garden.*]

DOCTOR: Mrs Venable?

MRS VENABLE: Yes?

DOCTOR: In your letter last week you made some reference to a, to a – fund of some kind, an endowment fund of –

MRS VENABLE: I wrote you that my lawyers and bankers and certified public accountants were setting up the Sebastian Venable Memorial Foundation to subsidize the work of young people like you that are pushing out the frontiers of art and science, but have a financial problem. You have a financial problem, don't you, Doctor?

DOCTOR: Yes, we do have that problem. My work is such a

new and *radical* thing that people in charge of state funds are
naturally a little scared of it and keep us on a small budget,
so small that – We need a separate ward for my patients, I
need trained assistants, I'd like to marry a girl I can't afford
to marry! – But there's also the problem of getting right
patients, not just – criminal psychopaths that the State turns
over to us for my operation! – because it's – well – risky. . . .
I don't want to turn you against my work at Lion's View,
but I have to be honest with you. There is a good deal of
risk in my operation. Whenever you enter the brain with a
foreign object . . .

MRS VENABLE: Yes.

DOCTOR: – Even a needle-thin knife . . .

MRS VENABLE: Yes.

DOCTOR: – In a skilled surgeon's fingers . . .

MRS VENABLE: Yes.

DOCTOR: – There is a good deal of risk involved in – the
operation. . . .

MRS VENABLE: You said that it pacifies them, it quiets them
down, it suddenly makes them peaceful.

DOCTOR: Yes. It does that, that much we already know, but –

MRS VENABLE: What?

DOCTOR: Well, it will be ten years before we can tell if the
immediate benefits of the operation will be lasting or –
passing or even if there'd still be – and this is what haunts
me about it! – any possibility, afterwards, of – reconstruct-
ing a – totally sound person, it may be that the person will
always be limited afterwards, relieved of acute disturbances
but – *limited*, Mrs Venable. . . .

MRS VENABLE: Oh, but what a blessing to them, Doctor, to
be just peaceful, to be just suddenly – peaceful. . . .
    [*A bird sings sweetly in the garden.*]
After all that horror, after those nightmares: just to be able
to lift up their eyes and see – [*She looks up and raises a hand
to indicate the sky.*] – a sky not as black with savage, devour-
ing birds as the sky that we saw in the Encantadas, Doctor.

DOCTOR: – Mrs Venable? I can't guarantee that a lobotomy
would stop her – *babbling*!!

MRS VENABLE: That may be, maybe not, but after the operation, who would *believe* her, Doctor?

[*Pause; faint jungle music.*]

DOCTOR [*quietly*]: My God.

[*Pause.*]

Mrs Venable, suppose after meeting the girl and observing the girl and hearing this story she babbles – I still shouldn't feel that her condition's – intractable enough! to justify the risks of – suppose I shouldn't feel that non-surgical treatment such as insulin shock and electric shock and –

MRS VENABLE: SHE'S HAD ALL THAT AT ST MARY'S!! Nothing else is left for her.

DOCTOR: But if I disagreed with you?

[*Pause.*]

MRS VENABLE: That's just part of a question: finish the question, Doctor.

DOCTOR: Would you still be interested in my work at Lion's View? I mean would the Sebastian Venable Memorial Foundation still be interested in it?

MRS VENABLE: Aren't we always more interested in a thing that concerns us personally, Doctor?

DOCTOR: Mrs Venable!!

[CATHARINE HOLLY *appears between the lace window curtains.*]

You're such an innocent person that it doesn't occur to you, it obviously hasn't even occurred to you that anybody less innocent than you are could possibly interpret this offer of a subsidy as – well, as sort of a *bribe*?

MRS VENABLE [*laughs, throwing her head back*]: Name it that – I don't care – There's just two things to remember. She's a destroyer. My son was a *creator*! – Now if my honesty's shocked you – pick up your little black bag without the subsidy in it, and run away from this garden! – Nobody's heard our conversation but you and I, Doctor Sugar....

[MISS FOXHILL *comes out of the house and calls.*]

MISS FOXHILL: Mrs Venable?

MRS VENABLE: What is it, what do you want, Miss Foxhill?

MISS FOXHILL: Mrs Venable? Miss Holly is here, with –
[MRS VENABLE *sees* CATHARINE *at the window.*]
MRS VENABLE: Oh, my God. There she is, in the window! –
I told you I didn't want her to enter my house again. I told
you to meet them at the door and lead them around the
side of the house to the garden, and you didn't listen. I'm
not ready to face her. I have to have my five o'clock cocktail first, to fortify me. Take my chair inside. Doctor? Are
you still here? I thought you'd run out of the garden. I'm
going back through the garden to the other entrance.
Doctor? Sugar? You may stay in the garden if you wish to
or run out of the garden if you wish to or go in this way if
you wish to or do anything that you wish to but I'm going
to have my five o'clock daiquiri, *frozen!* – before I face
her. . . .

[*All during this she has been sailing very slowly off through the
garden like a stately vessel at sea with a fair wind in her sails,
a pirate's frigate or a treasure-laden galleon. The young
* DOCTOR *stares at Catharine framed by the lace window curtains.*
SISTER FELICITY *appears beside her and draws her away
from the window. Music: an ominous fanfare.* SISTER FELICITY
holds the door open for Catharine as the DOCTOR *starts
quickly forward. He starts to pick up his bag, but doesn't.*
CATHARINE *rushes out, they almost collide with each other.*]
CATHARINE: Excuse me.
DOCTOR: I'm sorry. . . .
[*She looks after him as he goes into the house.*]
SISTER FELICITY: Sit down and be still till your family come
outside.

DIM OUT

SCENE TWO

[CATHARINE *removes a cigarette from a lacquered box on the
table and lights it. The following quick, cadenced lines are
accompanied by quick, dancelike movement, almost formal, as
the Sister in her sweeping white habit, which should be starched*

to make a crackling sound, pursues the girl about the white wicker patio table and among the wicker chairs: this can be accompanied by quick music.]

SISTER: What did you take out of that box on the table?

CATHARINE: Just a cigarette, Sister.

SISTER: Put it back in the box.

CATHARINE: Too late, it's already lighted.

SISTER: Give it here.

CATHARINE: Oh, please, let me smoke, Sister!

SISTER: Give it here.

CATHARINE: *Please*, Sister Felicity.

SISTER: Catharine, give it here. You know that you're not allowed to smoke at St Mary's.

CATHARINE: We're not at St Mary's, this is an afternoon out.

SISTER: You're still in my charge. I can't permit you to smoke because the last time you smoked you dropped a lighted cigarette on your dress and started a fire.

CATHARINE: Oh, I did not start a fire. I just burned a hole in my skirt because I was half unconscious under medication. *[She is now behind a white wicker chair.]*

SISTER *[overlapping her]*: Catharine, give it here.

CATHARINE: Don't be such a bully!

SISTER: Disobedience has to be paid for later.

CATHARINE: All right, I'll pay for it later.

SISTER *[overlapping]*: Give me that cigarette or I'll make a report that'll put you right back on the violent ward, if you don't. *[She claps her hands twice and holds one hand out across the table.]*

CATHARINE *[overlapping]*: I'm not being violent, Sister.

SISTER *[overlapping]*: Give me that cigarette, I'm holding my hand out for it!

CATHARINE: All right, take it, here, take it!

[She thrusts the lighted end of the cigarette into the palm of the Sister's hand. The SISTER cries out and sucks her burned hand.]

SISTER: *You burned me with it!*

CATHARINE: I'm sorry, I didn't mean to.

SISTER *[shocked, hurt]*: You deliberately burned me!

CATHARINE [*overlapping*]: You said give it to you and so I gave it to you.

SISTER [*overlapping*]: You stuck the lighted end of that cigarette in my hand!

CATHARINE [*overlapping*]: I'm *sick*, I'm *sick*! – of being *bossed* and *bullied*!

SISTER [*commandingly*]: *Sit down!*

[CATHARINE *sits down stiffly in a white wicker chair on fore-stage, facing the audience. The* SISTER *resumes sucking the burned palm of her hand. Ten beats. Then from inside the house the whirr of a mechanical mixer.*]

CATHARINE: There goes the Waring Mixer, Aunt Violet's about to have her five o'clock frozen daiquiri, you could set a watch by it! [*She almost laughs. Then she draws a deep, shuddering breath and leans back in her chair, but her hands remain clenched on the white wicker arms.*]

– We're in Sebastian's garden. *My God, I can still cry!*

SISTER: Did you have any medication before you went out?

CATHARINE: No. I didn't have any. Will you give me some, Sister?

SISTER [*almost gently*]: I can't. I wasn't told to. However, I think the doctor will give you something.

CATHARINE: The young blond man I bumped into?

SISTER: Yes. The young doctor's a specialist from another hospital.

CATHARINE: What hospital?

SISTER: A word to the wise is sufficient. . . .

[*The* DOCTOR *has appeared in the window.*]

CATHARINE [*rising abruptly*]: I knew I was being watched, he's in the window, staring out at me!

SISTER: Sit down and be still. Your family's coming outside.

CATHARINE [*overlapping*]: LION'S VIEW, IS IT! DOCTOR?

[*She has advanced toward the bay window. The* DOCTOR *draws back, letting the misty white gauze curtains down to obscure him.*]

SISTER [*rising with a restraining gesture which is almost pitying*]: Sit down, dear.

CATHARINE: IS IT LION'S VIEW? DOCTOR

SISTER: Be still. . . .

CATHARINE: WHEN CAN I STOP RUNNING DOWN THAT STEEP WHITE STREET IN CABEZA DE LOBO?

SISTER: Catharine, dear, sit down.

CATHARINE: I loved him, Sister! Why wouldn't he let me save him? I tried to hold on to his hand, but he struck me away and ran, ran, ran in the wrong direction, Sister!

SISTER: Catharine, dear – be still.

[*The* SISTER *sneezes.*]

CATHARINE: Bless you, Sister. [*She says this absently, still watching the window.*]

SISTER: Thank you.

CATHARINE: The Doctor's still at the window but he's too blond to hide behind window curtains, he catches the light, he shines through them. [*She turns from the window.*] – We were *going* to blonds, blonds were next on the menu.

SISTER: Be still now. Quiet, dear.

CATHARINE: Cousin Sebastian said he was famished for blonds, he was fed-up with the dark ones and was famished for blonds. All the travel brochures he picked up were advertisements of the blond northern countries. I think he'd already booked us to – Copenhagen or – Stockholm. – Fed up with dark ones, famished for light ones: that's how he talked about people, as if they were – items on a menu. – 'That one's delicious-looking, that one is appetizing,' or 'that one is *not* appetizing' – I think because he was really nearly half-starved from living on pills and salads. . . .

SISTER: *Stop it!* – Catharine, be still.

CATHARINE: He liked me and so I loved him. . . . [*She cries a little again.*] If he'd kept hold of my hand I could have saved him! – Sebastian suddenly said to me last summer: 'Let's fly north, little bird – I want to walk under those radiant, cold northern lights – I've never *seen* the aurora borealis!' – Somebody said once or wrote, once: 'We're all of us children in a vast kindergarten trying to spell God's name with the wrong alphabet blocks!'

MRS HOLLY [*offstage*]: *Sister?*

[*The* SISTER *rises.*]

CATHARINE [*rising*]: I think it's *me* they're calling, they call *me* 'Sister', Sister!

SCENE THREE

[*The* SISTER *resumes her seat impassively as the girl's mother and younger brother appear from the garden. The mother, Mrs Holly, is a fatuous Southern lady who requires no other description. The brother, George, is typically good-looking, he has the best 'looks' of the family, tall and elegant of figure. They enter.*]

MRS HOLLY: Catharine, dear! Catharine – [*They embrace tentatively.*] Well, well! Doesn't she look fine, George?

GEORGE: Uh huh.

CATHARINE: They send you to the beauty parlour whenever you're going to have a family visit. Other times you look awful, you can't have a compact or lipstick or anything made out of metal because they're afraid you'll swallow it.

MRS HOLLY [*giving a tinkly little laugh*]: I think she looks just splendid, don't you, George?

GEORGE: Can't we talk to her without the nun for a minute?

MRS HOLLY: Yes, I'm sure it's all right to. Sister?

CATHARINE: Excuse me, Sister Felicity, this is my mother, Mrs Holly, and my brother, George.

SISTER: How do you do.

GEORGE: How d'ya do.

CATHARINE: This is Sister Felicity. . . .

MRS HOLLY: We're so happy that Catharine's at St Mary's! So very grateful for all you're doing for her.

SISTER [*sadly, mechanically*]: We do the best we can for her, Mrs Holly.

MRS HOLLY: I'm sure you do. Yes, well – I wonder if you would mind if we had a little private chat with our Cathie?

SISTER: I'm not supposed to let her out of my sight.

MRS HOLLY: It's just for a minute. You can sit in the hall or

the garden and we'll call you right back here the minute
the private part of the little talk is over.

[SISTER FELICITY *withdraws with an uncertain nod and a
swish of starched fabric.*]

GEORGE [*to Catharine*]: *Jesus! What are you up to? Huh! Sister?
Are you trying to* RUIN *us?!*

MRS HOLLY: GAWGE! WILL YOU BE QUIET. You're up-
setting your sister!

[*He jumps up and stalks off a little, rapping his knee with his
zipper-covered tennis racket.*]

CATHARINE: How elegant George looks!

MRS HOLLY: George inherited Cousin Sebastian's wardrobe,
but everything else is in probate! Did you know that? That
everything else is in probate, and Violet can keep it in
probate just as long as she wants to?

CATHARINE: Where is Aunt Violet?

MRS HOLLY: *George, come back here!*

[*He does, sulkily.*]

Violet's on her way down.

GEORGE: Yeah, Aunt Violet has an elevator now.

MRS HOLLY: Yais, she has, she's had an elevator installed
where the back stairs were, and, Sister, it's the cutest little
thing you ever did see! It's panelled in Chinese lacquer,
black an' gold Chinese lacquer, with lovely bird-pictures
on it. But there's only room for two people at a time in it.
George and I came down on foot. – I think she's havin' her
frozen daiquiri now, she still has a frozen daiquiri promptly
at five o'clock ev'ry afternoon in the world . . . in warm
weather. . . . Sister, the horrible death of Sebastian just
about *killed* her! – She's now slightly better . . . but it's a
question of time. – Dear, you know, I'm sure that you
understand, why we haven't been out to see you at St
Mary's. They said you were too disturbed, and a family visit
might disturb you more. But I want you to know that
nobody, absolutely nobody in the city, knows a thing
about what you've been through. Have they, George? Not
a thing. Not a soul even knows that you've come back from
Europe. When people inquire, when they question us about

you, we just say that you've stayed abroad to study some-thing or other. [*She catches her breath.*] Now. Sister? – I want you to please be *very* careful what you say to your Aunt Violet about what happened to Sebastian in Cabeza de Lobo.

CATHARINE: What do you want me to say about what – ?

MRS HOLLY: Just don't repeat that same fantastic story! For my sake and George's sake, the sake of your brother and mother, don't repeat that horrible story again! Not to Violet! Will you?

CATHARINE: Then I am going to have to tell Aunt Violet what happened to her son in Cabeza de Lobo?

MRS HOLLY: Honey, that's why you're here. She has IN-SISTED on hearing it straight from YOU!

GEORGE: You were the only witness to it, Cathie.

CATHARINE: No, there were others. That *ran.*

MRS HOLLY: Oh, Sister, you've just had a little sort of a – *nightmare* about it! Now, listen to me, will you, Sister? Sebastian has left, has BEQUEATHED! – to you an' Gawge in his *will* –

GEORGE [*religiously*]: *To each of us, fifty grand, each!* – AFTER! TAXES! – GET IT?

CATHARINE: Oh, yes, but if they give me an injection – I won't have any choice but to tell exactly what happened in Cabeza de Lobo last summer. Don't you see? I won't have any choice but to tell the truth. It makes you tell the truth because it shuts something off that might make you able not to and *everything* comes out, decent or *not* decent, you have no control, but always, always the truth!

MRS HOLLY: Catharine, darling. I don't know the full story, but surely you're not too sick in your *head* to know in your *heart* that the story you've been telling is just – too –

GEORGE [*cutting in*]: Cathie, Cathie, you got to forget that story! Can'tcha? For *your* fifty grand?

MRS HOLLY: Because if Aunt Vi contests the will, and we know she'll contest it, she'll keep it in the courts for ever! – We'll be –

GEORGE: It's in PROBATE NOW! And'll never get out of probate until you drop that story – we can't afford to hire lawyers good enough to contest it! So if you don't stop telling that crazy story, we won't have a pot to – cook *greens* in!

[*He turns away with a fierce grimace and a sharp, abrupt wave of his hand, as if slapping down something.* CATHARINE *stares at his tall back for a moment and laughs wildly.*]

MRS HOLLY: Catharine, don't laugh like that; it scares me, Catharine.

[*Jungle birds scream in the garden.*]

GEORGE [*turning his back on his sister*]: Cathie, the money is all tied up.

[*He stoops over sofa, hands on flannel knees, speaking directly into* CATHARINE'*s face as if she were hard of hearing. She raises a hand to touch his cheek affectionately; he seizes the hand and removes it but holds it tight.*]

If Aunt Vi decided to contest Sebastian's will that leaves us all of this cash?! – Am I coming through to you?

CATHARINE: Yes, little brother, you are.

GEORGE: You see, Mama, she's crazy like a coyote! [*He gives her a quick cold kiss.*] We won't get a single damn penny, honest t' God we won't! So you've just GOT to stop tellin' that story about what you say happened to Cousin Sebastian in Cabeza de Lobo, even if it's what it *couldn't* be, TRUE! – You got to drop it, Sister, you can't tell such a story to civilized people in a civilized up-to-date country!

MRS HOLLY: Cathie, why, why, why! – did you invent such a tale?

CATHARINE: But, Mother, I DIDN'T invent it. I know it's a hideous story but it's a true story of our time and the world we live in and what did truly happen to Cousin Sebastian in Cabeza de Lobo....

GEORGE: Oh, then you are going to tell it. Mama, she IS going to tell it! Right to Aunt Vi, and lose us a hundred thousand! – Cathie? You are a BITCH!

MRS HOLLY: GAWGE!

GEORGE: I repeat it, a bitch! She isn't crazy, Mama, she's no

more crazy than I am, she's just, just – PERVERSE! Was
ALWAYS – perverse....

[CATHARINE *turns away and breaks into quiet sobbing.*]

MRS HOLLY: Gawge, Gawge, apologize to Sister, this is no
way for you to talk to your sister. You come right back
over here and tell your sweet little sister you're sorry you
spoke like that to her!

GEORGE [*turning back to* CATHARINE]: I'm sorry, Cathie, but
you know we NEED that money! Mama and me, we –
Cathie? I got *ambitions*! And, Cathie, I'm YOUNG! – I *want*
things, I *need* them, Cathie! So will you please think about
Me? Us?

MISS FOXHILL [*offstage*]: Mrs Holly? Mrs Holly?

MRS HOLLY: Somebody's callin' fo' me. Catharine, Gawge
put it very badly but you know that it's TRUE WE DO
HAVE TO GET WHAT SEBASTIAN HAS LEFT US IN HIS
WILL, DEAREST! AND YOU WON'T LET US DOWN?
PROMISE? YOU WON'T? LET US DOWN?

GEORGE [*fiercely shouting*]: HERE COMES AUNT VI! Mama,
Cathie, Aunt Violet's – here is Aunt Vi!

SCENE FOUR

[MRS VENABLE *enters downstage area. Entrance music.*]

MRS HOLLY: *Cathie! Here's Aunt Vi!*

MRS VENABLE: She sees me and I see her. That's all that's
necessary. Miss Foxhill, put my chair in this corner. Crank
the back up a little.

[MISS FOXHILL *does this business.*]

More. More. Not that much! – Let it back down a little.
All right. Now, then. I'll have my frozen daiquiri, now....
Do any of you want coffee?

GEORGE: I'd like a chocolate malt.

MRS HOLLY: Gawge!

MRS VENABLE: This isn't a drugstore.

MRS HOLLY: Oh, Gawge is just being Gawge.

MRS VENABLE: That's what I *thought* he was being!

[*An uncomfortable silence falls.* MISS FOXHILL *creeps out like a burglar. She speaks in a breathless whisper, presenting a cardboard folder to Mrs Venable.*]

MISS FOXHILL: Here's the portfolio marked Cabeza de Lobo. It has all your correspondence with the police there and the American Consul.

MRS VENABLE: I asked for the *English transcript*! It's in a separate –

MISS FOXHILL: Separate, yes, here it is!

MRS VENABLE: Oh . . .

MISS FOXHILL: And here's the report of the private investigators and here's the report of –

MRS VENABLE: Yes, yes, yes! Where's the doctor?

MISS FOXHILL: On the phone in the library!

MRS VENABLE: Why does he choose such a moment to make a phone call?

MISS FOXHILL: He didn't make a phone call. He received a phone call from –

MRS VENABLE: Miss Foxhill, why are you talking to me like a burglar?!

[MISS FOXHILL *giggles a little desperately.*]

CATHARINE: Aunt Violet, she's frightened. – Can I move? Can I get up and move around till it starts?

MRS HOLLY: Cathie, Cathie, dear, did Gawge tell you that he received bids from every good fraternity on the Tulane campus and went Phi Delt because Paul Junior did?

MRS VENABLE: I see that he had the natural tact and good taste to come here this afternoon outfitted from head to foot in clothes that belonged to my son!

GEORGE: You gave 'em to me, Aunt Vi.

MRS VENABLE: I didn't know you'd parade them in front of me, George.

MRS HOLLY [*quickly*]: Gawge, tell Aunt Violet how grateful you are for –

GEORGE: I found a little Jew tailor on Britannia Street that makes alterations so good you'd never guess that they weren't cut *out* for me to *begin* with!

MRS HOLLY: AND so reasonable! – Luckily, since it seems that Sebastian's wonderful, wonderful bequest to Gawge an' Cathie is going to be tied up a while!?

GEORGE: Aunt Vi? About the will?

[MRS HOLLY *coughs*.]

I was wondering if we can't figure out some way to, to –

MRS HOLLY: Gawge means to EXPEDITE it! To get through the red tape quicker?

MRS VENABLE: I understand his meaning. Foxhill, get the Doctor.

[*She has risen with her cane and hobbled to the door.*]

MISS FOXHILL [*exits calling*]: Doctor!

MRS HOLLY: Gawge, no more about money.

GEORGE: How do we know we'll ever see her again?

[CATHARINE *gasps and rises; she moves downstage, followed quickly by* SISTER FELICITY.]

SISTER [*mechanically*]: What's wrong, dear?

CATHARINE: I think I'm just dreaming this, it doesn't seem real!

MISS FOXHILL [*comes back out*]: He had to answer an urgent call from Lion's View.

[*Slight, tense pause.*]

MRS HOLLY: Violet! *Not* Lion's View!

[SISTER FELICITY *had started conducting Catharine back to the patio; she stops her now*.]

SISTER: Wait, dear.

CATHARINE: What for? I know what's coming.

MRS VENABLE [*at same time*]: Why? Are you all prepared to put out a thousand a month plus extra charges for treatments to keep the girl at St Mary's?

MRS HOLLY: Cathie? Cathie, dear?

[CATHARINE *has returned with the* SISTER.]

Tell Aunt Violet how grateful you are for her makin' it possible for you to rest an' recuperate at such a sweet, sweet place as St Mary's!

CATHARINE: No place for lunatics is a sweet, sweet place.

MRS HOLLY: But the food's good there. Isn't the food good there?

CATHARINE: Just give me written permission not to eat fried grits. I had yard privileges till I refused to eat fried grits.

SISTER: She lost yard privileges because she couldn't be trusted in the yard without constant supervision or even with it because she'd run to the fence and make signs to cars on the highway.

CATHARINE: Yes, I did, I did that because I've been trying for weeks to get a message out of that 'sweet, sweet place'.

MRS HOLLY: What message, dear?

CATHARINE: I got panicky, Mother.

MRS HOLLY: Sister, I don't understand.

GEORGE: What're you scared of, Sister?

CATHARINE: What they might do to me now, after they've done all the rest! – That man in the window's a specialist from Lion's View! We get newspapers. I know what they're ...

[*The* DOCTOR *comes out.*]

MRS VENABLE: Why, Doctor, I thought you'd left us with just that little black bag to remember you by!

DOCTOR: Oh, no. Don't you remember our talk? I had to answer a call about a patient that –

MRS VENABLE: This is Dr Cukrowicz. He says it means 'sugar' and we can call him 'Sugar' –

[GEORGE *laughs.*]

He's a specialist from Lion's View.

CATHARINE [*cutting in*]: WHAT DOES HE SPECIALIZE IN?

MRS VENABLE: Something new. When other treatments have failed.

[*Pause. The jungle clamour comes up and subsides again.*]

CATHARINE: *Do you want to bore a hole in my skull and turn a knife in my brain?* Everything else was done to me!

[MRS HOLLY *sobs.* GEORGE *raps his knee with the tennis racket.*]

You'd have to have my mother's permission for that.

MRS VENABLE: I'm paying to keep you in a private asylum.

CATHARINE: You're not my legal guardian.

MRS VENABLE: Your mother's dependent on me. All of you are! – Financially. . . .

CATHARINE: I think the situation is – clear to me, now. . . .

MRS VENABLE: Good! In that case. . . .

DOCTOR: I think a quiet atmosphere will get us the best results.

MRS VENABLE: I don't know what you mean by a quiet atmosphere. She shouted, I didn't.

DOCTOR: Mrs Venable, let's try to keep things on a quiet level, now. Your niece seems to be disturbed.

MRS VENABLE: She has every reason to be. She took my son from me, and then she –

CATHARINE: Aunt Violet, you're not being fair.

MRS VENABLE: Oh, aren't I?

CATHARINE [to the others]: She's not being fair. [Then back to Mrs Venable] Aunt Violet, you know why Sebastian asked me to travel with him.

MRS VENABLE: Yes, I *do* know why!

CATHARINE: You weren't able to travel. You'd had a – [She stops short.]

MRS VENABLE: Go on! *What* had I had? Are you afraid to say it in front of the Doctor? She meant that I had a stroke. – I DID NOT HAVE A STROKE! – I had a slight aneurism. You know what that is, Doctor? A little vascular convulsion! Not a haemorrhage, just a little convulsion of a blood-vessel. I had it when I discovered that she was trying to take my son away from me. Then I had it. It gave a little temporary – muscular – contraction. – To one side of my face. . . . [She crosses back into main acting area.] These people are not blood-relatives of mine, they're my dead husband's relations. I always detested these people, my dead husband's sister and – her two worthless children. But I did more than my duty to keep their heads above water. To please my son, whose weakness was being excessively softhearted, I went to the expense and humiliation, yes, public humiliation, of giving this girl a début which was a fiasco. Nobody liked her when I brought her out. Oh, she had some kind of – notoriety! She had a sharp tongue that some people

139

mistook for wit. A habit of laughing in the faces of decent people which would infuriate them, and also reflected adversely on me and Sebastian, too. But, he, Sebastian, was amused by this girl. While I was disgusted, sickened. And halfway through the season, she was dropped off the party lists, yes, dropped off the lists in spite of my position. Why? Because she'd lost her head over a young married man, made a scandalous scene at a Mardi Gras ball, in the middle of the ballroom. Then everybody dropped her like a hot – rock, but – [*She loses her breath.*] My son, Sebastian, still felt sorry for her and took her with him last summer instead of me. . . .

CATHARINE [*springing up with a cry*]: I can't change truth. I'm not God! I'm not even sure that He could, I don't think God can change truth! How can I change the story of what happened to her son in Cabeza de Lobo?

MRS VENABLE [*at the same time*]: She was in love with my son!

CATHARINE [*overlapping*]: Let me go back to St Mary's. Sister Felicity, let's go back to Saint –

MRS VENABLE [*overlapping*]: Oh, no! That's not where you'll go!

CATHARINE [*overlapping*]: All right. *Lion's View*, but don't ask me to –

MRS VENABLE [*overlapping*]: You *know* that you were!

CATHARINE [*overlapping*]: That I was *what*, Aunt Violet?

MRS VENABLE [*overlapping*]: Don't call me 'Aunt'. You're the niece of my dead husband, not me!

MRS HOLLY [*overlapping*]: Catharine, Catharine, don't upset your – Doctor? Oh, Doctor!

[*But the* DOCTOR *is calmly observing the scene with detachment. The jungle garden is loud with the sounds of its feathered and scaled inhabitants.*]

CATHARINE: I don't want to, I didn't want to come here! I know what she thinks, she thinks I murdered her son, she thinks that I was responsible for his death.

MRS VENABLE: That's right. I told him when he told me that he was going with you in my place last summer that I'd never see him again and I never did. And only you know why!

CATHARINE: Oh, my God, I –

[*She rushes out toward garden, followed immediately by the* SISTER.]

SISTER: Miss Catharine, Miss Catharine –

DOCTOR [*overlapping*]: Mrs Venable?

SISTER [*overlapping*]: Miss Catharine?

DOCTOR [*overlapping*]: Mrs Venable?

MRS VENABLE: What?

DOCTOR: I'd like to be left alone with Miss Catharine for a few minutes.

MRS HOLLY: George, talk to her, George.

[GEORGE *crouches appealingly before the old lady's chair, peering close into her face, a hand on her knee.*]

GEORGE: Aunt Vi? Cathie can't go to Lion's View. Everyone in the Garden District would know you'd put your niece in a state asylum, Aunt Vi.

MRS VENABLE: Foxhill!

GEORGE: What do you want, Aunt Vi?

MRS VENABLE: Let go of my chair. Foxhill? Get me away from people!

GEORGE: Aunt Vi, listen, think of the talk it –

MRS VENABLE: I can't get up! Push me, push me away!

GEORGE [*rising, but holding chair*]: I'll push her, Miss Foxhill.

MRS VENABLE: Let go of my chair or –

MISS FOXHILL: Mr Holly, I –

GEORGE: I got to talk to her.

[*He pushes her chair downstage.*]

MRS VENABLE: Foxhill!

MISS FOXHILL: Mr Holly, she doesn't want you to push her.

GEORGE: I know what I'm doing. Leave me alone with Aunt Vi!

MRS VENABLE: Let go me or I'll *strike* you!

GEORGE: Oh, Aunt Vi!

MRS VENABLE: Foxhill!

MRS HOLLY: George –

GEORGE: Aunt Vi?

[*She strikes at him with her cane. He releases the chair and* MISS FOXHILL *pushes her off. He trots after her a few steps, then he returns to* MRS HOLLY, *who is sobbing into a handkerchief. He sighs, and sits down beside her, taking her hand. The scene fades as light is brought up on* CATHARINE *and the* SISTER *in the garden. The* DOCTOR *comes up to them.* MRS HOLLY *stretches her arms out to* GEORGE, *sobbing, and he crouches before her chair and rests his head in her lap. She strokes his head. During this: the* SISTER *has stood beside Catharine, holding on to her arm.*]

CATHARINE: You don't have to hold on to me. I can't run away.

DOCTOR: Miss Catharine?

CATHARINE: What?

DOCTOR: Your aunt is a very sick woman. She had a stroke last spring?

CATHARINE: Yes, she did, but she'll never admit it...

DOCTOR: You have to understand why.

CATHARINE: I do. I understand why. I didn't want to come here.

DOCTOR: Miss Catharine, do you hate her?

CATHARINE: I don't understand what hate is. How can you hate anybody and still be sane? You see, I still think I'm sane!

DOCTOR: You think she did have a stroke?

CATHARINE: She had a slight stroke in April. It just affected one side, the left side, of her face ... but it was disfiguring and, after that, Sebastian couldn't use her.

DOCTOR: Use her? Did you say use her?

[*The sounds of the jungle garden are not loud but ominous.*]

CATHARINE: Yes, we all use each other and that's what we think of as love, and not being able to use each other is what's – *hate.* ....

DOCTOR: Do you hate her, Miss Catharine?

CATHARINE: Didn't you ask me that, once? And didn't I say that I didn't understand hate. A ship struck an iceberg at sea – everyone sinking –

DOCTOR: Go on, Miss Catharine!

CATHARINE: But that's no reason for everyone drowning for hating everyone drowning! Is it, Doctor?

DOCTOR: Tell me: what was your feeling for your cousin Sebastian?

CATHARINE: He liked me and so I loved him.

DOCTOR: In what way did you love him?

CATHARINE: The only way he'd accept: – a sort of motherly way. I tried to save him, Doctor.

DOCTOR: From what? Save him from what?

CATHARINE: Completing! – sort of! – *image!* – he had of himself as a sort of! – *sacrifice* to a! – *terrible* sort of a –

DOCTOR: – God?

CATHARINE: Yes, a – *cruel* one, Doctor!

DOCTOR: How did you feel about that?

CATHARINE: Doctor, my feelings are the sort of feelings that you have in a dream. . . .

DOCTOR: Your life doesn't seem real to you?

CATHARINE: Suddenly last winter I began to write my journal in the third person.

[*He grasps her elbow and leads her out upon forestage. At the same time* MISS FOXHILL *wheels* MRS VENABLE *off,* MRS HOLLY *weeps into a handkerchief, and* GEORGE *rises and shrugs and turns his back to the audience.*]

DOCTOR: Something happened last winter?

CATHARINE: At a Mardi Gras ball some – some boy that took me to it got too drunk to stand up! [*A short, mirthless note of laughter.*] I wanted to go home. My coat was in the cloakroom, they couldn't find the check for it in his pockets. I said, 'Oh, hell, let it go!' – I started out for a taxi. Somebody took my arm and said, 'I'll drive you home.' He took off his coat as we left the hotel and put it over my shoulders, and then I looked at him and – I don't think I'd ever even seen him before then, really! – He took me home in his car, but took me another place first. We stopped near the Duelling Oaks at the end of Esplanade Street. . . . Stopped! – I said, 'What for?' – He didn't answer, just struck a match in the car to light a cigarette in the car and I looked at him in the car and I knew 'what for'! – I think I got out of the car before he got out of the car, and we walked through the wet grass to the great misty oaks as if somebody was calling us for help there!

[*Pause. The subdued, toneless bird-cries in the garden turn to a single bird-song.*]

DOCTOR: After that?

CATHARINE: I lost him. – He took me home and said an awful thing to me. 'We'd better forget it,' he said, 'my wife's expecting a child and –' – I just entered the house and sat there thinking a little and then I suddenly called a taxi and went right back to the Roosevelt Hotel ballroom. The ball was still going on. I thought I'd gone back to pick up my borrowed coat, but that wasn't what I'd gone back for. I'd gone back to make a scene on the floor of the ballroom, yes, I didn't stop at the cloakroom to pick up Aunt Violet's old mink stole, no, I rushed right into the ballroom and spotted him on the floor and ran up to him and beat him as hard as I could in the face and chest with my fists till – Cousin Sebastian took me away. – After that, the next morning, I started writing my diary in the third person, singular, such as 'She's still living this morning', meaning that *I* was. . . . 'WHAT'S NEXT FOR HER? GOD KNOWS!' – I couldn't go out any more. – However, one morning my Cousin Sebastian came in my bedroom and said: 'Get up!' – Well . . . if you're still alive after dying, well then, you're obedient, Doctor. – I got up. He took me downtown to a place for passport photos. Said: 'Mother can't go abroad with me this summer. You're going to go with me this summer instead of Mother.' – If you don't believe me, read my journal of Paris! – 'She woke up at daybreak this morning, had her coffee, and dressed and took a brief walk –'

DOCTOR: *Who* did?

CATHARINE: *She* did. *I* did – from the Hotel Plaza Athénée to the Place de l'Étoile as if pursued by a pack of Siberian wolves! [*She laughs her tired, helpless laugh.*] – Went right through all stop signs – couldn't wait for green signals. – 'Where did she think she was going? Back to the Duelling

Oaks?' – Everything chilly and dim but his hot, ravenous mouth! on –

DOCTOR: Miss Catharine, let me give you something.

[*The others go out, leaving* CATHARINE *and the* DOCTOR *onstage.*]

CATHARINE: Do I have to have the injection again, this time? What am I going to be stuck with this time, Doctor? I don't care. I've been stuck so often that if you connected me with a garden hose I'd make a good sprinkler.

DOCTOR [*preparing needle*]: Please take off your jacket.

[*She does. The* DOCTOR *gives her an injection.*]

CATHARINE: I didn't feel it.

DOCTOR: That's good. Now sit down.

[*She sits down.*]

CATHARINE: Shall I start counting backwards from a hundred?

DOCTOR: Do you like counting backwards?

CATHARINE: Love it! Just love it! One hundred! Ninety-nine! Ninety-eight! Ninety-seven! Ninety-six. Ninety – five – Oh! – I already feel it! How funny!

DOCTOR: That's right. Close your eyes for a minute.

[*He moves his chair closer to hers. Half a minute passes.*]

Miss Catharine? I want you to give me something.

CATHARINE: Name it and it's yours, Doctor Sugar.

DOCTOR: Give me all your resistance.

CATHARINE: Resistance to what?

DOCTOR: The truth. Which you're going to tell me.

CATHARINE: The truth's the one thing I have never resisted!

DOCTOR: Sometimes people just think they don't resist it, but still do.

CATHARINE: They say it's at the bottom of a bottomless well, you know:

DOCTOR: Relax.

CATHARINE: Truth.

DOCTOR: Don't talk.

CATHARINE: Where was I, now? At ninety?

DOCTOR: You don't have to count backwards.

CATHARINE: At ninety something?

DOCTOR: You can open your eyes.

CATHARINE: Oh, I do feel funny!

[*Silence, pause.*]

You know what I think you're doing? I think you're trying to hypnotize me. Aren't you? You're looking so straight at me and doing something to me with your eyes and your – eyes. . . . Is that what you're doing to me?

DOCTOR: Is that what you *feel* I'm doing?

CATHARINE: Yes! I feel so peculiar. And it's not just the drug.

DOCTOR: Give me all your resistance. See. I'm holding my hand out. I want you to put yours in mine and give me all your resistance. Pass all of your resistance out of your hand to mine.

CATHARINE: Here's my hand. But there's no resistance in it.

DOCTOR: You are totally passive.

CATHARINE: Yes, I am.

DOCTOR: You will do what I ask.

CATHARINE: Yes, I will try.

DOCTOR: You will tell the true story.

CATHARINE: Yes, I will.

DOCTOR: The absolutely true story. No lies, nothing not spoken. Everything told, exactly.

CATHARINE: Everything. Exactly. Because I'll have to. Can I – can I stand up?

DOCTOR: Yes, but be careful. You might feel a little bit dizzy.

[*She struggles to rise, then falls back.*]

CATHARINE: I can't get up! Tell me to. Then I think I could do it.

DOCTOR: Stand up.

[*She rises unsteadily.*]

CATHARINE: How funny! Now I can! Oh, I do feel dizzy! Help me, I'm –

[*He rushes to support her.*]

– about to fall over. . . .

[*He holds her. She looks out vaguely toward the brilliant, steaming garden. Looks back at him. Suddenly sways toward him, against him.*]

DOCTOR: You see, you lost your balance.

CATHARINE: No, I didn't. I did what I wanted to do without you telling me to. [*She holds him tight against her.*] Let me! Let! Let! Let me! Let me, let me, oh, let me. . . . [*She crushes her mouth to his violently. He tries to disengage himself. She presses her lips to his fiercely, clutching his body against her. Her brother* GEORGE *enters.*] Please hold me! I've been so lonely. It's lonelier than death, if I've gone mad, it's lonelier than death!

GEORGE [*shocked, disgusted*]: *Cathie!* – you've got a hell of a nerve.

[*She falls back, panting, covers her face, runs a few paces and grabs the back of a chair.* MRS HOLLY *enters.*]

MRS HOLLY: What's the matter, George? Is Catharine ill?

GEORGE: No.

DOCTOR: Miss Catharine had an injection that made her a little unsteady.

MRS HOLLY: What did he say about Catharine?

[CATHARINE *has gone out into the dazzling jungle of the garden.*]

SISTER [*returning*]: She's gone into the garden.

DOCTOR: That's all right. She'll come back when I call her.

SISTER: It may be all right for you. You're not responsible for her.

[MRS VENABLE *has re-entered.*]

MRS VENABLE: Call her now!

DOCTOR: Miss Catharine! Come back. [*To the Sister*] Bring her back, please, Sister!

[CATHARINE *enters quietly, a little unsteady.*]

Now, Miss Catharine, you're going to tell the true story.

CATHARINE: Where do I start the story?

DOCTOR: Wherever you think it started.

CATHARINE: I think it started the day he was born in this house.

MRS VENABLE: Ha! You see!

GEORGE: Cathie.

DOCTOR: Let's start later than that.

[*Pause.*]

Shall we begin with last summer?

CATHARINE: Oh. Last summer.

DOCTOR: Yes. Last summer.

[*There is a long pause. The raucous sounds in the garden fade into a bird-song which is clear and sweet.* MRS HOLLY *coughs.* MRS VENABLE *stirs impatiently.* GEORGE *crosses downstage to catch Catharine's eye as he lights a cigarette.*]

CATHARINE: Could I – ?

MRS VENABLE: Keep that boy away from her!

GEORGE: She wants to smoke, Aunt Vi.

CATHARINE: Something helps in the – hands. . . .

SISTER: Unh unh!

DOCTOR: It's all right, Sister. [*He lights her cigarette.*] About last summer: how did it begin?

CATHARINE: It began with his kindness and the six days at sea that took me so far away from the – Duelling Oaks that I forgot them, nearly. He was affectionate with me, so sweet and attentive to me, that some people took us for a honeymoon couple until they noticed that we had – separate state-rooms, and – then in Paris, he took me to Patou and Schiaparelli's – *this* is from Schiaparelli's! [*Like a child, she indicates her suit.*] – bought me so many new clothes that I gave away my old ones to make room for my new ones in my new luggage to – travel. . . . I turned into a peacock! Of course, so was *he* one, too. . . .

GEORGE: *Ha ha!*

MRS VENABLE: Shh!

CATHARINE: But then I made the mistake of responding too much to his kindness, of taking hold of his hand before he'd take hold of mine, of holding on to his arm and leaning on his shoulder, of appreciating his kindness more than he wanted me to, and, suddenly last summer, he began to be restless, and – oh!

DOCTOR: Go on.

CATHARINE: The Blue Jay notebook!

DOCTOR: Did you say notebook?

MRS VENABLE: I know what she means by that. She's talking about the school composition book with a Blue Jay trademark that Sebastian used for making notes and revisions on his 'Poem of Summer'. It went with him everywhere that he went, in his jacket pocket, even his dinner jacket. I have the one that he had with him last summer. *Foxhill! The Blue Jay notebook!*

[MISS FOXHILL *rushes in with a gasp.*]

It came with his personal effects shipped back from Cabeza de Lobo.

DOCTOR: I don't quite get the connexion between new clothes and so forth and the Blue Jay notebook.

MRS VENABLE: I HAVE IT! – Doctor, tell her I've found it.

[MISS FOXHILL *hears this as she comes back out of house: gasps with relief, retires.*]

DOCTOR: With all these interruptions it's going to be awfully hard to –

MRS VENABLE: This is important. I don't know why she mentioned the Blue Jay notebook, but I want you to see it. Here it is, here! [*She holds up a notebook and leafs swiftly through the pages.*] Title? 'Poem of Summer', and the date of the summer – 1935. After that: *what? Blank pages, blank pages,* nothing but *nothing!* – last summer. . . .

DOCTOR: What's that got to do with – ?

MRS VENABLE: His destruction? I'll tell you. A poet's vocation is something that rests on something as thin and fine as the web of a spider, Doctor. That's all that holds him *over!* – out of destruction. . . . Few, very few are able to do it alone! Great help is needed. I *did* give it! She *didn't*.

CATHARINE: She's right about that. I failed him. I wasn't able to keep the web from – breaking. . . . I saw it breaking but couldn't save or – repair it!

MRS VENABLE: There now, the truth's coming out. We had an agreement between us, a sort of contract or covenant between us which he broke last summer when he broke away from me and took her with him, not me! When he was frightened and I knew when and what of, because his hands would shake and his eyes looked in, not out, I'd reach across a table and touch his hands and say not a word, just look, and touch his hands with my hand until his hands stopped shaking and his eyes looked out, not in, and in the morning, the poem would be continued. *Continued until it was finished!*

[*The following ten speeches are said very rapidly, overlapping.*]

CATHARINE: I – couldn't!

MRS VENABLE: *Naturally* not! He was *mine*! I *knew* how to help him, I *could*! You didn't, you couldn't!

DOCTOR: These interruptions –

MRS VENABLE: I would say 'You *will*' and he *would*, I – !

CATHARINE: Yes, you see, I failed him! And so, last summer, we went to Cabeza de Lobo, we flew down there from where he gave up writing his poem last summer. . . .

MRS VENABLE: Because he'd broken our –

CATHARINE: Yes! Yes, something had broken, that string of pearls that old mothers hold their sons by like a – sort of a – sort of – *umbilical* cord, *long – after* . . .

MRS VENABLE: She means that I held him back from —

DOCTOR: *Please!*

MRS VENABLE: *Destruction!*

CATHARINE: All I know is that suddenly, last summer, he wasn't young any more, and we went to Cabeza de Lobo, and he suddenly switched from the evenings to the beach. . . .

DOCTOR: From evenings? To beach?

CATHARINE: I mean from the evenings to the afternoons and from the fa – fash –

[*Silence.* MRS HOLLY *draws a long, long painful breath.* GEORGE *stirs impatiently.*]

DOCTOR: Fashionable! Is that the word you – ?

CATHARINE: Yes. Suddenly, last summer Cousin Sebastian changed to the afternoons and the beach.

DOCTOR: What beach?

CATHARINE: In Cabeza de Lobo there is a beach that's named for Sebastian's name saint, it's known as La Playa San Sebastian, and that's where we started spending all afternoon, every day.

DOCTOR: What kind of beach was it?

CATHARINE: It was a big city beach near the harbour.

DOCTOR: It was a big public beach?

CATHARINE: Yes, public.

MRS VENABLE: It's little statements like that that give her away.

[*The* DOCTOR *rises and crosses to* MRS VENABLE *without breaking his concentration on Catharine.*]

After all I've told you about his fastidiousness, can you accept such a statement?

DOCTOR: You mustn't interrupt her.

MRS VENABLE [*overlapping him*]: That Sebastian would go every day to some dirty free public beach near a harbour? A man that had to go out a mile in a boat to find water fit to swim in?

DOCTOR: Mrs Venable, no matter what she says, you have to let her say it without any more interruptions or this interview will be useless.

MRS VENABLE: I won't speak again. I'll keep still, if it kills me.

CATHARINE: I don't want to go on....

DOCTOR: Go on with the story. Every afternoon last summer your Cousin Sebastian and you went out to this free public beach?

CATHARINE: No, it wasn't the free one, the free one was right next to it, there was a fence between the free beach and the one that we went to that charged a small charge of admission.

DOCTOR: Yes, and what did you do there?

[*He still stands beside Mrs Venable and the light gradually changes as the girl gets deeper into her story: the light concentrates on Catharine, the other figures sink into shadow.*]

Did anything happen there that disturbed you about it?

CATHARINE: Yes!

DOCTOR: What?

CATHARINE: He bought me a swim-suit I didn't want to wear. I laughed. I said, 'I can't wear that. It's a scandal to the jaybirds!'

DOCTOR: What did you mean by that? That the suit was immodest?

CATHARINE: My God, yes! It was a one-piece suit made of white lisle, the water made it transparent! [*She laughs sadly at the memory of it.*] – I didn't want to swim in it, but he'd grab my hand and drag me into the water, all the way in, and I'd come out looking naked!

DOCTOR: Why did he do that? Did you understand why?

CATHARINE: Yes! To attract! – Attention.

DOCTOR: He wanted you to attract attention, did he, because he felt you were moody? Lonely? He wanted to shock you out of your depression last summer?

CATHARINE: Don't you understand? I was PROCURING for him!

[MRS VENABLE'S *gasp is like the sound that a great hooked fish might make.*]

She used to do it, *too*.

[MRS VENABLE *cries out.*]

Not consciously! She didn't *know* that she was procuring for him in the smart, the fashionable places they used to go to before last summer! Sebastian was shy with people. She wasn't. Neither was I. We both did the same thing for him, made contacts for him, but she did it in nice places and in decent ways and I had to do it the way that I just told you! – Sebastian was lonely, Doctor, and the empty Blue Jay notebook got bigger and bigger, so big it was big and empty as that big empty blue sea and sky. . . . I knew what I was doing. I came out in the French Quarter years before I came out in the Garden District. . . .

MRS HOLLY: Oh, Cathie! Sister . . .

DOCTOR: Hush!

CATHARINE. And before long, when the weather got warmer and the beach so crowded, he didn't need me anymore for that purpose. The ones on the free beach began to climb over the fence or swim around it, bands of homeless young people that lived on the free beach like scavenger dogs, hungry children. . . . So now he let me wear a decent dark suit. I'd go to a faraway empty end of the beach, write postcards and letters and keep up my – third-person journal till it was – five o'clock and time to meet him outside the bathhouses, on the street.... He would come out, *followed*.

DOCTOR: Who would follow him out?

CATHARINE: The homeless, hungry young people that had climbed over the fence from the free beach that they lived on. He'd pass out tips among them as if they'd all – shined his shoes or called taxis for him.... Each day the crowd was bigger, noisier, greedier! – Sebastian began to be frightened. – At last we stopped going out there....

DOCTOR: And then? After that? After you quit going out to the public beach?

CATHARINE: Then one day, a few days after we stopped going out to the beach – it was one of those white blazing days in Cabeza de Lobo, not a blazing hot *blue* one but a blazing hot *white* one.

DOCTOR: Yes?

CATHARINE: We had a late lunch at one of those open-air restaurants on the sea there. – Sebastian was white as the weather. He had on a spotless white silk Shantung suit and a white silk tie and a white panama and white shoes, white – white lizard skin – pumps! He – [*She throws back her head in a startled laugh at the recollection.*] – kept touching his face and his throat here and there with a white silk handkerchief and popping little white pills in his mouth, and I knew he was having a bad time with his heart and was frightened about it and that was the reason we hadn't gone out to the beach....

[*During the monologue the lights have changed, the surrounding area has dimmed out and a hot white spot is focused on Catharine.*]

'I think we ought to go north,' he kept saying, 'I think we've done Cabeza de Lobo, I think we've done it, don't you?' *I* thought we'd done it! – but I had learned it was better not to seem to have an opinion because if I did, well, Sebastian, well, you know Sebastian, he always preferred to do what no one else wanted to do, and I always tried to give the impression that I was agreeing reluctantly to his wishes ... it was a – game....

SISTER: She's dropped her cigarette.

DOCTOR: I've got it, Sister.

[*There are whispers, various movements in the penumbra. The* DOCTOR *fills a glass for her from the cocktail-shaker.*]

CATHARINE: Where was I? Oh, yes, that five o'clock lunch at one of those fish-places along the harbour of Cabeza de Lobo, it was between the city and the sea, and there were naked children along the beach which was fenced off with barbed wire from the restaurant and we had our table less than a yard from the barbed-wire fence that held the beggars at bay.... There were naked children along the beach, a band of frightfully thin and dark naked children that looked a flock of plucked birds, and they would come darting up to the barbed-wire fence as if blown there by the wind, the hot white wind from the sea, all crying out, '*Pan, pan, pan!*'

DOCTOR [*quietly*]: What's *pan*?

CATHARINE: The word for bread, and they made gobbling noises with their little black mouths, stuffing their little black fists to their mouths and making those gobbling noises, with frightful grins! – Of course we were sorry that we had come to this place, but it was too late to go....

DOCTOR [*quietly*]: Why was it 'too late to go'?

CATHARINE: I told you Cousin Sebastian wasn't well. He was popping those little white pills in his mouth. I think he had popped in so many of them that they had made him feel weak.... His, his! – eyes looked – dazed, but he said: 'Don't look at those little monsters. Beggars are a social disease in this country. If you look at them, you get sick of the country, it spoils the whole country for you....'

DOCTOR: Go on.

CATHARINE: I'm going on. I have to wait now and then till it gets clearer. Under the drug it has to be a vision or nothing comes....

DOCTOR: All right?

CATHARINE: Always when I was with him I did what he told me. I didn't look at the band of naked children, not even when the waiters drove them away from the barbed-wire fence with sticks! – Rushing out through a wicket gate like

an assault party in war! – and beating them screaming away
from the barbed-wire fence with the sticks. . . . Then!
   [*Pause.*]

DOCTOR: Go on, Miss Catharine, what comes next in the
vision?

CATHARINE: The, the the! – band of children began to –
serenade us. . . .

DOCTOR: Do what?

CATHARINE: Play for us! On instruments! Make music! – if
you could call it music. . . .

DOCTOR: Oh?

CATHARINE: Their, their – instruments were – instruments
of percussion! – Do you know what I mean?

DOCTOR [*making a note*]: Yes. Instruments of percussion such
as – *drums?*

CATHARINE: I stole glances at them when Cousin Sebastian
wasn't looking, and as well as I could make out in the white
blaze of the sand-beach, the instruments were tin cans
strung together.

DOCTOR [*slowly, writing*]: Tin – cans – strung – together.

CATHARINE: *And, and, and, and – and!* – bits of metal, *other* bits
of metal that had been flattened out, made into –

DOCTOR: What?

CATHARINE: *Cymbals!* You know? *Cymbals?*

DOCTOR: Yes. Brass plates hit together.

CATHARINE: That's right, Doctor. – Tin cans flattened out
and clashed together! – Cymbals. . . .

DOCTOR: Yes. I understand. What's after that, in the vision?

CATHARINE [*rapidly, panting a little*]: And others had paper
bags, bags made out of – coarse paper! – with something on
a string inside the bags which they pulled up and down,
back and forth, to make a sort of a –

DOCTOR: Sort of a – ?

CATHARINE: Noise like –

DOCTOR: Noise like?

CATHARINE [*rising stiffly from chair*]: Ooompa! Ooompa!
Ooooooompa!

DOCTOR: Ahhh . . . a sound like a *tuba?*

CATHARINE: That's right! – they made a sound like a
tuba....

DOCTOR: Oompa, oompa, oompa, like a tuba.
[*He is making a note of the description.*]

CATHARINE: Oompa, oompa, oompa, like a –
[*Short pause.*]

DOCTOR: – Tuba....

CATHARINE: All during lunch they stayed at a – a fairly *close*
– *distance....*

DOCTOR: Go on with the vision, Miss Catharine.

CATHARINE [*striding about the table*]: *Oh, I'm going on, nothing
could stop it now!!*

DOCTOR: Your Cousin Sebastian was *entertained* by this –
concert?

CATHARINE: I think he was *terrified* of it!

DOCTOR: Why was he terrified of it?

CATHARINE: I think he recognized some of the musicians,
some of the boys, between childhood and – older....

DOCTOR: What did he do? Did he do anything about it, Miss
Catharine? – Did he complain to the manager about it?

CATHARINE: *What* manager? *God?* Oh, no! – The manager
of the fishplace on the beach? Ha ha! – No! – You don't
understand my cousin!

DOCTOR: What do you mean?

CATHARINE: *He! – accepted! – all! –* as – how! – things! – are!
– And thought nobody had any right to complain or inter-
fere in any way whatsoever, and even though he knew that
what was awful was awful, that what was wrong was
wrong, and my Cousin Sebastian was certainly never sure
that anything was wrong! – He thought it unfitting to ever
take any action about anything whatsoever! – except to go
on doing as something in him directed....

DOCTOR: What did something in him direct him to do? – I
mean on this occasion in Cabeza de Lobo.

CATHARINE: After the salad, before they brought the coffee,
he suddenly pushed himself away from the table, and said,
'They've got to stop that! Waiter, make them stop that.
I'm not a well man, I have a heart condition, it's making me

sick!' – This was the first time that Cousin Sebastian had ever attempted to correct a human situation! – I think perhaps that *that* was his – fatal error.... It was then that the waiters, all eight or ten of them, charged out of the barbed-wire wicket gate and beat the little musicians away with clubs and skillets and anything hard that they could snatch from the kitchen! – Cousin Sebastian left the table. He stalked out of the restaurant after throwing a handful of paper money on the table and he fled from the place. I followed. It was all white outside. White hot, a blazing white hot, hot blazing white, at five o'clock in the afternoon in the city of – Cabeza de Lobo. It looked as if –

DOCTOR: It looked as if?

CATHARINE: As if a huge white bone had caught on fire in the sky and blazed so bright it was white and turned the sky and everything under the sky white with it!

DOCTOR: White ...

CATHARINE: Yes – white ...

DOCTOR: You followed your Cousin Sebastian out of the restaurant on to the hot white street?

CATHARINE: Running up and down hill....

DOCTOR: You ran up and down hill?

CATHARINE: No, no! *Didn't* – move either *way*! – at first, we were –

[*During this recitation there are various sound effects. The percussive sounds described are very softly employed.*]

I rarely made any suggestion, but *this* time I *did*....

DOCTOR: What did you suggest?

CATHARINE: Cousin Sebastian seemed to be paralysed near the entrance of the café, so I said, 'Let's go.' I remember that it was a very wide and steep white street, and I said, 'Cousin Sebastian, down that way is the waterfront and we are more likely to find a taxi near there.... Or why don't we go back in? – and have them *call* us a taxi! Oh, let's do! Let's do *that*, that's better!' And he said, '*Mad*, are you *mad*? Go back in that filthy place? Never! That gang of kids shouted vile things about me to the waiters!' 'Oh,' I said, 'then let's go down toward the docks, down there at the bottom of the hill, let's not try to climb the hill in this dreadful heat.' And Cousin Sebastian shouted, 'Please shut up, let me handle this situation, will you? I want to handle this thing.' And he started up the steep street with a hand stuck in his jacket where I knew he was having a pain in his chest from his palpitations... But he walked faster and faster, in panic, but the faster he walked the louder and closer it got!

DOCTOR: What got louder?

CATHARINE: The music.

DOCTOR: The music again.

CATHARINE: The oompa-oompa of the – following band. – They'd somehow gotten through the barbed wire and out on the street, and they were following, following! – up the blazing white street. The band of naked children pursued us up the steep white street in the sun that was like a great white bone of a giant beast that had caught on fire in the sky! – Sebastian started to run and they all screamed at once and seemed to fly in the air, they outran him so quickly. I screamed. I heard Sebastian scream, he screamed just once before this flock of black plucked little birds that pursued him and overtook him halfway up the white hill.

DOCTOR: And you, Miss Catharine, what did *you* do, then?

CATHARINE: Ran!

DOCTOR: Ran where?

CATHARINE: Down! Oh, I ran down, the easier direction to run was down, down, down, down! – The hot, white, blazing street, screaming out 'Help' all the way, till –

DOCTOR: What?

CATHARINE: – Waiters, police, and others – ran out of buildings and rushed back up the hill with me. When we got back to where my Cousin Sebastian had disappeared in the flock of featherless little black sparrows, he – he was lying naked as they had been naked against a white wall, and this you won't believe, nobody *has* believed it, nobody *could* believe it, nobody, nobody on earth could possibly believe it, and I don't *blame* them! – They had *devoured* parts of him.

[MRS VENABLE *cries out softly.*]

158

Torn or cut parts of him away with their hands or knives or maybe those jagged tin cans they made music with, they had torns bits of him away and stuffed them into those gobbling fierce little empty black mouths of theirs. There wasn't a sound any more, there was nothing to see but Sebastian, what was left of him, that looked like a big white-paper-wrapped bunch of red roses had been *torn, thrown, crushed!* – against that blazing white wall. . . .

[MRS VENABLE *springs with amazing power from her wheelchair, stumbles erratically but swiftly toward the girl and tries to strike her with her cane. The* DOCTOR *snatches it from her and catches her as she is about to fall. She gasps hoarsely several times as he leads her toward the exit.*]

MRS VENABLE [*offstage*]: *Lion's View! State asylum, cut this hideous story out of her brain!*

[MRS HOLLY *sobs and crosses to* GEORGE, *who turns away from her.*]

GEORGE: Mom, I'll quit school, I'll get a job, I'll –

MRS HOLLY: Hush, son! Doctor, can't you say something?

[*Pause. The* DOCTOR *comes downstage.* CATHARINE *wanders out into the garden, followed by the* SISTER.]

DOCTOR [*after a while, reflectively, into space*]: I think we ought at least to consider the possibility that the girl's story could be true. . . .